DAMIAN

by

Alan Robert Ward

Copyright © Alan Robert Ward 2009

ISBN: 978-1-4452-1040-7

Printed & Published by Lulu
3131 RDU Centre, Suite 235
Morrisville, North Carolina, 27560; USA

Distributed by Oberon Ventures
Suite 78, 55 Griva Digeni Street
8220, Chloraka, Pafos, Cyprus

WARNING

This book contains items

of an ADULT nature

including graphic descriptions

of young male homosexual sex

It is not meant to offend

and is based on a true story

One

"Damian, why don't you just do as you are told. You're old enough now to know better."

"Why should I?"

"Because I say so, that's why."

"At least I'm nearly sixteen. Then I can do whatever I like!"

"Not in this house you can't. While you are living here under this roof, you'll do as you are told and like it!" Mrs Fordham moved towards the lounge door. "I suggest that you use the next three weeks to sort yourself out, young man. While you continue to behave like a child, you will be treated like one. Thank goodness your brother doesn't behave like you and never did when he was your age."

She left the room leaving Damian to think about what she had said. His mother just couldn't understand what had got into him these last few months, although deep down, she knew that something had seemed to happen to him just after his fourteenth birthday. That's when she thought that he had begun to change. Yes, Mrs Fordham had already been through that stage with Daniel, Damian's older brother, but he had never been as rebellious as Damian was now. She just couldn't understand why he should change so dramatically.

To the rest of the world, Damian was just another rebellious teenager, growing up in the mid 1990's with all of the peer pressure that existed. He did look much younger than his fifteen years and forty-nine weeks, having grown to the height of five feet and four inches, yet he retained the looks of a thirteen year old boy.

As yet, there was no sign of him having reached

the stage in his development whereby, he would find that the daily wash had to be followed by dragging a razor across those precious baby-like features.

What really annoyed Damian most was that being the youngest member of the family, he regularly got the blame for all of his elder brothers 'practical jokes'. Daniel has just turned eighteen and seemed to be forever telling his younger brother that he was a man and, that Damian would never reach the same definition of the word. A form of ritual-like teasing that goes on in many families between brothers and sisters but, this was meant. Daniel was not a person to glibly pass comments that he did not mean. Perhaps it was the venom in his eyes that gave Damian the impression that the joking that had accompanied such remarks in the past, had all but stopped.

Despite all of their togetherness years, Damian did begin to feel the deep hurt and malice behind or contained in all of his brothers remarks. He looked for it too in all of his parents pontificating. Any love that may have built up over the years was now fading fast with their relationship turning to nothing more than pure tolerance of each other.

All his parents could do was to sit back and watch their baby boy grow up into, in their eyes, the connotation of his name. That in itself prompted much teasing at school. His fellow pupils who all professed to be friends, would almost continuously look for that sign. The three sixes in his hair. Showers proved to be an additional problem when the whole of his body seemed to be probed and prodded by these so called friends.

Try as they might, both John and Linda Fordham could not seem to accept the fact that Damian was growing up, albeit, not as quickly as Daniel had done. Love was there in abundance, but was visually prevented

from being shown to Damian on many of the occasions that they did try to show it. This was because of the solitude that Damian had seemed to have chosen for himself recently, and the disturbing fact that he had just seemed to switch off from the world around him. A classic sign of a young boy with adolescence related problems in addition to coping with the physical and mental transition from boyhood to manhood that now seemed to beset his young body.

Quite often his parents found themselves discussing the problems relating to Damian's adolescence. In today's culture, so many parents use this important stage of change and growing up, to hide under the carpet, the truth. It is usually used as an excuse to save parents from looking at an obvious problem. The easy way out being used so that they do not have to face the problems which exist and thereby, avoiding the confrontation that would automatically ensue.

The two brothers used to get on very well. All through their early childhood they would play together and at times, seemed to be inseparable. The rot began to set in just after Damian's thirteenth birthday. This coincided with him joining his brother at the local comprehensive school. Understandably Daniel - who had started that school two years earlier - had by now begun to collect his own fairly wide circle of friends and had started that summer to go out in the evenings and at weekends with them, rather than with Damian.

Daniel had begun to develop his own identity too and quite naturally, didn't want 'little brother' tagging along. This left Damian out on a limb and in some ways, became the first catalyst relating to his present precarious behaviour. Perhaps for the first time in his life, Damian had to learn to get along without his brother for

companionship and support. Indeed, on the occasions when Damian found himself caught up in what are frequently described as 'playground scraps', big brother was content to let the proceedings continue with no thought for his brother's pain, suffering or even embarrassment.

This gave Damian an element of freedom and independence, both were things that he had never had the benefit of in the past. Although he was a fairly extrovert boy, he had since the age of fourteen, started to become very introvert and withdrawn. He became very secretive, very devious and, instead of forming his own large circle of friends like his elder brother had quite successfully done, he began to alienate most of those seeking his friendship; tending to stick to two or three friends, and rapidly, turning into a loner.

This didn't bother Daniel because like his parents, he also assumed that the changes within Damian, were due to the hormone changes in his body, coupled with his physical adolescent development. It was however not the case, and if anything, it was big brother Daniel who had been the second catalyst in the saga of events leading to his younger brothers downfall.

It was the third Wednesday afternoon of the long six week school summer holidays and as had become usual by now, Damian was in his bedroom listening to some music through his headphones. He was not aware of anything around him, nor the fact that his brother and a friend were in Daniel's bedroom. This was not really an exceptional occurrence because quite often, Daniel would have friends in and they would either talk, play music or watch a video. A privilege that Damian was not permitted except on very rare occasions. On this occasion Damian removed his headphones from his stereo before turning

down the volume, and resulted in Daniel thumping the dividing wall between their bedrooms, followed by several choice words of abuse.

Damian had reached the point where he had decided not to take any more of his brother's abuse, so foolishly, he decided to go into Daniel's room to have it out with him. His brothers aggressive attitude had made Damian see red. Deep down he knew that if they were to fight, either physically or verbally he would lose, but this didn't deter him from confronting Daniel. As he opened the door and stormed in, he was not ready for the sight that greeted him.

Both Daniel and his friend James were laying on Daniel's bed, stark naked It became very obvious even to the young naive Damian exactly what had been going on. Far from beating a hasty retreat, Damian went into the room and closed the door behind him. The sight that greeted him had already prevented him from having a row with his brother, and he now saw a golden opportunity for him to be able to get some revenge. He began to smile and giggle as Daniel spoke.

"What do you want? Piss off!" he said very aggressively.

"Don't know," Damian replied somewhat gingerly. Yes, he had heard the banging on the wall but the sight that had greeted him now just made him freeze. He couldn't have moved, even if he wanted to. He was also quite intrigued, wanting to know more, and exactly what had been going on - just in case his suspicions were incorrect.

"We weren't doing anything," Daniel added whilst ensuring that pillows now covered both James' and his own embarrassment.

"No we weren't," James added.

"Anyway," Daniel said smirking and looking at James. "Nothing more than you do every night!"

The two boys began to laugh uncontrollably. This really annoyed Damian and he retaliated in the only way that he knew.

"I shan't tell anyone. In any case, I haven't seen anything that small for years!" Knowing that he definitely wouldn't get away with such a comment, he began to beat a hasty retreat to the bedroom door. Daniel and James quickly jumped up from the bed to prevent Damian from escaping. He could have had no idea about the ordeal that was to follow.

"Get off me," he cried as the two boys dragged him over to the bed. "I'll tell!" he said; trying to escape from their ever tightening grasp. James and Daniel looked at each other.

"Do you think that anyone would believe you if you did tell? You're such a liar, nobody will." Damian had no intention of putting up with that abuse.

"I ain't a liar!"

"Is that so?"

"Yes."

"Well, you've just lied to us."

"When?"

"Just now."

"How?"

"How? I'll tell you. You said that you hadn't seen anything so small for years." James began to smirk.

"So?"

"Well, I'll show you something much smaller than what we've got and, it ain't been years since you've seen it."

Daniel pushed his brother down onto the bed so that he was lying flat on his back. James grabbed

Damian's arms and held him very tight while Daniel began to part his brother from his trousers and boxer shorts. Although he squirmed and fought, it was only a matter of seconds before Damian was completely naked, still being held down by both boys.

All three looked at each other once Damian had finally stopped struggling. He needed no help to become as erect as his captors, indicating as far as they were concerned, and his willingness to join in whatever they had in mind. He knew that he was not going to be left out, not now that he was as naked and as erect as they were. James grabbed Damian's hand and placed it upon his own throbbing tool. As he did so, Daniel knelt down between Damian's legs, grabbing his brothers' cock, while allowing a smile to cross his face. This was met with a smile from James but trepidation from Damian.

"Kneel up," James said to Damian. "You can hold it better that way." As he did so, he exchanged glances with Daniel. It was the look that said it all. Damian knew that the initial excitement that he may have shown to the two boys and by giving up the fight too easily, not only seemed to indicate to his captors, his willingness to participate in whatever they had planned but, also his anticipated enjoyment of what could happen. He now began to feel very insecure and unsure of himself and, of them.

James positioned himself in front of Damian and after a few seconds, gradually moved nearer to him so that his cock was only a matter of inches away from Damian's mouth. While he did this, Daniel continued to wank his brother, moving ever closer until from time to time, his own erect cock touched his brothers' tight arse. The first time that this happened, Damian looked around and realised that the inevitable was about to happen and,

that there was nothing that he could do to stop it. He was totally at their mercy.

First, he began to feel his brother's finger gently move inside him. As it did so, James moved Damian's hand away from his cock and held his head tightly as he gently pushed his cock into Damian's mouth.

"Suck it," demanded James. "Suck harder!" With his head quite firmly held, he could do no more than to obey. He only had about two inches in his mouth but began to suck on it as best he could. He was quite relieved when Daniel removed his finger but, the respite lasted only a few seconds before Daniel's eight inch hard cock was being pushed inside him. Damian moaned and this had the effect of allowing James to push more of his own cock inside Damian's mouth.

The ordeal lasted about ten minutes after which time, James exploded into the youngsters mouth. Having made sure that every drop had been swallowed, he released Damian's head and began to wank him. He didn't have long to wait. Almost at the same time that Daniel shot his hot load deep into his brother, it was their victims turn to produce.

"That's what cheeky young boys get," Daniel said as he withdrew his cock from his brother's arse.

"You won't tell now, will you?" James added.

"No," whispered Damian.

"That's not very convincing you little runt, was it Dan?"

"Not really."

"Let's make sure."

James gestured to Daniel and they changed places. In the hope that his ordeal was finally over, Damian had turned over onto his back.

first time and, was again sworn to secrecy.

"If you tell anyone that you've done it to me," Daniel said; "then I'll make sure that you'll never do it to anyone ever again." Damian agreed even though deep down, he was still frightened, just in case the abuse got any worse. He could just about put up with the current level but, didn't trust his brother just in case it did get worse.

Damian was younger, yes; but not quite as naive when it came to sexual matters as perhaps his brother had thought. He knew that Daniel used to brag to his mates that he had been the first one to fuck that tender young virgin arse. When the abuse first began during the summer holidays and unbeknown to his brother, Damian had already become quite sexually experienced.

He had for the last year or so, passed an element of his spare time at the local youth club. All went well and he took an active part in all of the activities offered. He was quite nervous at first because it was time that the two brothers had chosen different ways in which to spend their leisure time.

It was spring and just before his thirteenth birthday. Together with about twenty or so other boys and girls, he began to go on the youth clubs weekly outing to the local swimming baths. When it finally came to get dried and changed, there tended to be a rush to occupy the changing cubicles. On one occasion as he entered through one door of a cubicle, another boy entered the same cubicle through the other door, Neither boy would leave so they decided to share.

The practice of sharing cubicles although not encouraged was not actively discouraged either, despite the fact that it was somewhat cramped. Damian knew the other boy who was fifteen at that time and had at junior

his relationship with either Mark or Jason affect him. He knew of other boys at school who were doing the same thing but, apart from the occasional hand job in the school toilets, he never got too involved with them, despite the fact that pocket money used to change hands.

During their sex education lessons at school, it had been pointed out that these forms of relationships do occur in young boys, and are nothing more than adolescent experimentation and sexual awareness. He too at first, put his rapidly growing interest in this form of sexual activity down to the same criteria. He knew that as long as he kept quiet about it, neither Mark or Jason would say anything either. Indeed, none of his partners would say anything because they too, would be revealed.

With Daniel it was very different. He never felt that it was right. There seemed something dirty about having any form of sexual contact with his brother or for that matter. his brother's friends. Almost all of Daniel's friends treated it really as a joke. Damian didn't.

It was purely that series of sessions that really caused him to become so withdrawn, moody and rebellious. He would often lay awake at night wondering why he ever went into Daniel's room on that first day. Perhaps if he hadn't then, his adolescence and the rest of his life, would have turned out very different.

Despite all of that, he knew that the situation at home was becoming intolerable. He knew that once he became sixteen, then he would be free to do as he liked. He could even leave home if he wished. If he did decide to leave, what would he do, where would he go, how would he survive?

His eyes began to feel heavy as he lay in bed contemplating his future. He knew all too well that the abuse that he was suffering both physical and mental

would continue while he remained resident at home, or until Daniel left, and there was little prospect of that happening in the foreseeable future.   There was no girlfriend on the horizon. In his eyes, there could be only one solution. He must leave home and would need to spend some time over the next three weeks planning this. He knew that it wouldn't be easy. The journey would be fraught with many dangers and full of uncertainty.

Somewhat contented, he finally slept.

Two

The next three weeks seemed to Damian as if they would never end. It was as if at every turn that he tried to make, that it was met with obstacle after obstacle. Would he ever achieve his ambition and fulfil his decision to leave the torture of his home? Still to be decided upon was, where to go, when to go, and most important of all, what would he do when he got there.

Damian withdrew from his family even more. He would appear for meals and, instead of spending the evenings with his family, would either seek the solitude of his bedroom or, of course spend time with Jason.

All his waking hours were spent dreaming of the day when he could wish his family farewell. Deep down, he knew that all the important questions had still to be answered. He knew that despite his desperate wish just to walk out of his home and to go, he would have to lay down a plan of action. Thinking about what he would take or leave behind were of course important but, he still had to decide where to go, when to go, how he would get there and, even more importantly, where would he live and what sort of job could be get in order to buy food and to pay for his accommodation. The one thing that he knew that he wouldn't be able to cope with was, either the fact or prospect of having to sleep rough in some bus shelter, doorway or park bench.

Damian had just left Jason's house on the Thursday evening following a fairly steamy session. Knowing that it was getting late - almost nine-thirty - he decided to take a short cut from the back of his friends house, across the park and he would hope to sneak into his house without being heard. He knew only too well that his

parents would be at him upon his arrival home for being late. Nine o'clock was the curfew during school time unless he was out with them or, it was a very special occasion. As far as they were concerned, tonight did not fall into either category.

As he crossed the park, he noticed the children's swings at one end of the park. He made straight for them, totally unconcerned now about time. He seemed just to need a bit of time on his own. He sat lonely on a swing and began to rock slowly backwards and forwards. All the world seemed to be upon him.

It was then that he slowly began to witness reality. How could he leave home? Would he be able to cope if he did actually leave? Surely it wouldn't be difficult, would it? His dreams began to fade. His world suddenly shattered by all of the practicalities of leaving the secure family nest, where if nothing else, he at least had an element of protection.

Having finally convinced himself that the only alternative before him was to leave the comforts of the family home, a few tears began to run down his sad young face. He looked up at the clear blue sky as if he was waiting for a bolt of inspiration to descend upon him. Is there a God? If there is, then perhaps he would take pity on him and show him what to do and which way to go. Surely he does care and is all knowledgeable. No inspiration was forthcoming.

As he slowly lowered his head, he noticed two older lads walking along one side of the park. It was too dark by now for him to be able to see who they were, but he noticed that they disappeared from sight, quite close to a small building that was in the far corner of the park. He hadn't even noticed its existence before but somehow, didn't find the event strange at first. After what seemed to

be only a couple of minutes, one of the lads walked away from the building and out of the park. He looked for the other lad but there was no sign of him, presuming that he had perhaps left the park by another route.

Dusk was now beginning to settle and Damian knew that he must go home soon, despite the wrath that he surely knew would be awaiting him when he did. As he got down from the swing, his curiosity began to get the better of him, and he began to walk towards the building in the corner of the park. As he got much closer to it, he could see that it was a public toilet block and thought to himself that he may as well make use of the facilities while he was there. It would after all, save him the embarrassment of having to find a bush to go behind on the way home. He checked that he was going into the right one then, he walked in.

Once his task was completed, he turned from the urinal and realised that he was not alone in there. The other lad who he had seen earlier was still there, It gave him quite a shock but thought it better to speak to him.

"Hi. It's dark in here," he said.

"Yeah. Can't see a bloody thing. Nearly pissed on my shoes," the lad replied.

"Didn't know that this place was here. Usually find a bush on the way home."

"No? Still, just as well. It beats pissing up a wall, yeah?"

"Yeah."

Damian's eyes were by now, beginning to get used to the dark and the outline of the urinals and of the other lad were coming more and more into focus. As the conversation continued, the lad turned slightly giving Damian a full view of what he had to offer.

"Got the time, mate?" the lad enquired. Damian tried to look at his watch but it was too dark. "I've got a match," the lad said as he moved towards Damian. He held the match over Damian's watch which allowed Damian to see that the time was ten minutes to ten and also, gave him a good view of the erect cock displayed before him. Damian blew out the match but made no effort to move, neither did his new found friend.

"You can if you like," the lad whispered to Damian.

Damian didn't need asking a second time and his hand reached out to feel the other lads waiting equipment, and after a few hand movements he could not only feel his own cock becoming erect but a hand desperately searching for it. Once unzipped, the lad suggested that they went into a cubicle to continue what they had started. Damian readily agreed.

Shortly after Damian had felt the older boy's hot rod deep inside him, he heard footsteps outside. They began to get closer and closer until two people came into the building. Damian listened intently for the footsteps to fade as quickly as they had arrived but, this was not to be. Slowly the cubicle door began to open and there stood two lads of about eighteen years of age. As they watched, Damian knew that although they were there for the same reason as his new found friend, they were not about to make use of the cubicle next door. Instead they decided just to wait their turn and because at that moment he was currently getting a good nine inches pounding away inside him, he knew only too well that he was to be their next target. He made no attempt to leave.

The two boys looked at each other and without any hesitation, unzipped themselves, securing each other's erection and began to move ever closer until their cocks

were touching Damian's eager lips. Like a baby feeding from a bottle, he opened his lips and began to suck each of them in turn. As he feared, both his eager holes were filled by hot ejaculations, in turn. Before they left, one of the lads forced a piece of paper into Damian's hand. He wasn't sure what it was so he put it into his pocket and waited until the light from a street light revealed that it was a ten pound note.

Upon his arrival home just before midnight, his parents were waiting up for him to arrive.

"What time do you call this?" his mother said. "We've been worried sick."

Damian did not reply or even acknowledge their presence. Instead, he went straight upstairs to his room, got into bed and went straight to sleep. He knew that he had only postponed the ordeal because they would be waiting for him in the morning, but surely he thought; they wouldn't be that hard on him - not on his sixteenth birthday. He could now have the freedom whenever he wanted and whenever he had both the courage and the resources to leave. Oh how he had been waiting for this day.

When he woke the following morning, there were no cards put by his bedside. No one came into his room to wish him happy birthday, so he realised that as his presents were usually placed by his breakfast place in the kitchen then, they must be there. People had been asking him what he would like and without exception, replied that he wanted cash. He had spun them a yarn about buying a new stereo and was going to put the money towards that, but deep down, he knew that he would need as much cash as possible if he was to fulfil his dream and finally leave home.

While he slowly began to make is way downstairs, he glanced over the banister and could hear that his mother and brother were discussing his late night out. If he went into the kitchen now, he would have been got at so, having made the decision to skip breakfast, quickly put on his coat and left the house by the front door as quietly as he could. By the time his mother would have realised that he had again escaped her wrath, and then it would be too late.

What would he do now? He didn't fancy spending the day at school so, he began to walk towards Jason's house. He knew that Jason wouldn't be there but also knew that he would have to pass the park where if the truth were to be known, he had spent an enjoyable hour or so the night before. Upon arriving at the park he made straight for the swings. This would give him the opportunity of being able to watch the comings and goings without getting too close. Shortly after his arrival he saw the cleaners arrive and subsequently leave. All was quiet but it was still only nine-thirty in the morning. Plenty of time, he thought.

As he sat waiting, his thoughts were dominated by his wish to leave home. It was all very well in theory to plan his great escape from the perils of his family, because up until now, theory was all that he had. Having finally reached the age where his parents could not stop him leaving or indeed could choose to throw him out on his ear, was very different. He knew that the next time that his parents challenged a decision that he had made or for that matter, had given him an instruction that he did not keep, he would threaten to leave home and his pride would ensure that he did just that. That would force him to make decisions very quickly, but with the overriding desire

already to leave home, he would not let such a technicality prevent him from reaching his goal.

He swung backwards and forwards. Eyes closed and a small tear began to run down his childish face, reality had begun to set in. Could he just pack a bag and leave in the middle of the night? He would have to sleep somewhere and would have to get himself a job to pay for all the food and clothing that he would need. He knew that he couldn't rely on the odd five or ten pounds being handed out every time that he touched his toes for someone else's pleasure, or could he.

Damian began to slowly open his eyes and looked down the park. He visualised running across the grass, desperate to get to the other side but however much he tried, he could not reach the end. There was no sanctuary in sight, no privacy at home. What was he to do?

It began to rain quite heavily and Damian made straight for the toilet block for shelter. He had never been there during the day before and spent quite some time reading all of the graffiti in the two cubicles. Footsteps. He nervously but quickly closed the cubicle door and sat down. The footsteps seemed to get nearer and then he heard someone go into the other cubicle.

There was a piece of toilet paper hanging on the wall which he removed only to find that a large hole had been made in the wall by someone, and that he could see straight through into the other cubicle. The other person was standing up and was in full view of Damian's eager eye. As he watched, he felt a strong stirring in his own groin and within less than a minute, Damian too was erect. He could tell that the other person was not much older than himself and when they took the opportunity of looking through at him, he made sure that they wouldn't

be disappointed. His door slowly opened and a boy of about seventeen stood there. Damian fully opened the door so that the boy could come in.

No payment ensued this time although he knew that if he stayed there long enough, someone would surely give him some money for 'services rendered'. There was soon another sound of footsteps, this time much younger. He could hear the person urinating and when they had finished, there were no footsteps leaving the building. As he sat there wondering if he should make himself known to the youngster, the cubicle door began to open slowly. Damian was sitting facing the door, his trousers around his knees, cock in hand. The other boy who was only about thirteen just stood there watching, the bulge in his jeans getting bigger by the minute. Damian beckoned for him to come in and the boy nervously entered. He had never met anyone quite that young who had obviously gained more experience than himself, and despite a nervous start, the young boy seemed determined that this encounter would indeed be a two way process. Once the rain had stopped, Damian went back to the swings to continue his thoughts and dreams.

By lunchtime there had been two more encounters. After each, Damian returned to the comparative safety and freedom that he found on the swing. One eye ever trained on the toilet block, the other looking around for some inspiration and guidance about his immediate future. Deep down he knew that there would be no sound of bells pointing his way in life as it did for Dick Whittington but, if he was going to leave home and go away to find his own fame and fortune then, now was the time. There was no point in putting off the decision any more.

Damian had spent the past few weeks dreaming about the day that he would finally pluck up enough courage to leave the sanctuary of his home and begin to make his own way in the world. Why shouldn't he? It would have to be now, or never. That he knew. Tomorrow, he would not have the courage to go. He began to smile with relief at having made his mind up and although he knew that he might regret the decision, it had finally been made. There would be no turning back.

It was then that he saw someone coming towards him. At first he thought that it might be Daniel. Perhaps he had found out that his younger brother had skived off school and had come looking for him. This made him very tense. As the boy got nearer, he realised that it wasn't his elder brother but that it was his friend, Jason.

"Hi," Damian said getting off the swing to greet him.

"Hi," Jason replied. "Not at school?"

"What? On my birthday? No chance!"

"What's wrong?"

"Nothing. Why?"

"You seem as if a weight has been lifted off you. More cheerful than you've been for ages."

"Something like that. Anyway. Why are you skiving off?"

"It was only games this afternoon so once everyone else had changed, I slipped out of the back gate and legged it.

"Oh."

"Much happening?" Jason asked as his eyes fell on the building in the corner of the park.

"Where?" Damian replied innocently.

"In the bogs. You've not taken your eyes off the place since I've been here."

"Oh." Damian wasn't too happy about being found out but realised that Jason must also use the toilets, so it wasn't so bad once he'd had the chance to think about it. "Would you do me a favour?"

"If I can."

"I need to get some stuff from home while the place is empty. Would you give us a hand?"

"Yeah. Now?" Damian looked at his watch.

"Yeah. The old girl will be back in an hour or so, so we'll have to be quick."

Both boys headed off to Damian's home and during their walk, Damian began to decide which of his clothes that he would take with him and what he would be forced to leave behind. He knew that he could only take with him what he could carry, and that it wouldn't be very much at all.

Once four large bags had been packed to capacity, Damian dashed downstairs to collect the cheques and cash that had been left for him in the kitchen. He horridly scribbled a note to say that he would telephone in a few days and that his family were not to worry. He took one brief look at the kitchen and then left.

The boys headed straight for Jason's house where Damian promised that he would tell his friend exactly what was going on. Well, Jason was shell-shocked. He insisted that he made Damian something to eat while he took a quick shower. He knew that what Damian had told him was in confidence and that he would not be able to tell anyone else. That placed a burden upon him but, it was one that he was quite happy to carry, for his friend.

Once Damian had showered and eaten, the two boys hugged each other knowing that it may be some time before they would meet again. Tears began to run down both their innocent faces. Damian looked at his watch. He still had time to get away before his parents or brother got home and read his note so, with a fond farewell, Damian left for the railway station. He had no idea of where he would go but felt that it needed to be some distance from home.

When he finally arrived at the railway station, he began to look at the railway timetable to see exactly what trains were running that day and where he could get a train to. London was his first thought but he had seen on so many television programmes the plight of the homeless on the streets of the capital. Perhaps the seaside, he thought. Nervously, he waited his turn in the queue at the ticket office and it was then that he began to read some of the advertising posters. He saw one showing Blackpool Tower. Surely that would be a good place to go, and there would be plenty of opportunity to get a job with all of the extra holiday workers the town needed. There would be guesthouses in abundance and he knew that he should be able to get a room without too much trouble.

He was soon on his way. In four hours time he would be looking at the sea. A far better prospect than staying at home to be shouted at or to be abused. As he boarded the train, there was a tear. Only a small one, but a tear nevertheless. He would miss his friends but as the train pulled out of the station, he nevertheless began to plan his life and indeed, his future existence.

What would await him in the phallic Northwest?

Three

Some thirty minutes after leaving Coventry station, the train pulled into Birmingham New Street where he knew that he would have to change trains. Damian managed to successfully get all of his luggage off the train, and then he made his way to a different platform, where he waited for the Preston train to arrive. It was some thirty minutes or so before it was due so, he decided to seek some refreshment and then manhandled all his belongings into the platform coffee bar to wait, only to find that it was a no smoking areas as indeed, was the remainder of the station. Making do with a large can of cola, he patiently waited. The doubts then began to set in. He could just turn round and get a train back home, or press onward to where he hoped his dreams could be fulfilled.

He had never been to Blackpool before and had only ever seen pictures of it on television. The lights, the Pleasure Beach, the Big One. What on earth could be in store. He knew about the famous Blackpool Tower recently celebrated its centenary and about the famous Blackpool Pleasure Beach with its new roller coaster. It didn't tell him much about the town that he was now proposing to seek fame and fortune in.

His thoughts were thankfully interrupted by the Preston train pulling into the station and he quickly made his way to the smoking coach and sat down to enjoy the two and three-quarter hour journey. The train pulled out and he was on his way. There was no going back now. All he could do now was to sit back and enjoy the journey.

He wasn't taking too much notice of the countryside or of the other passengers as he was listening

to some music on his personal stereo. Once the Take That tape had finished, he rummaged though one of his bags to find another cassette tape. It didn't have a label on it so he thought that he'd play it anyway. It was a tape of a Jimmy Somerville CD and the first track was Smalltown Boy. How appropriate the words were. *"You leave in the morning with everything you own in a little black case. Alone on a platform. Mother will never understand why you had to leave. For the love that you need will never be found at home, always a lonely boy."*

It related to leaving home for the bright lights, getting away to make a new start. It couldn't have been more appropriate but it did cause a tear or two to slowly run down his baby face. As he wiped it away, he glanced up and noticed another boy of about his age coming out of the toilet and sit at the table on the other side of the gangway. Damian smiled at him, closed his eyes, and let the full meaning of the music sink in.

He drifted off to sleep for about an hour and only just woken in time to hear the announcement saying that Preston station was the next stop. He hurriedly gathered together his luggage and then made for the carriage door ready to alight. As the train pulled in there were not many people about. Strange, he thought but, managed to get off before the train went on its way. Now all he had to do was to find out which platform the train to Blackpool North went from. It meant crossing under the tracks but he knew that he had plenty of time to catch the train that would take him on the final leg of his journey. After all, he was on the journey to the rest of his life.

There were about twenty people waiting on the platform and right at the far end of the platform, he noticed the young lad who had sat opposite him on the train from Birmingham. Perhaps he hadn't just been to the

toilet and had just walked down the train to find the smoking coach. No matter. All he could think about now was getting on the train, and to travel off to the new life that lay ahead; this time taking note of the countryside and looking for Blackpool's famous phallus.

Time was getting on and as he looked at his watch, he realised that it was almost seven o'clock. Would he be able to get somewhere to sleep when he finally got to Blackpool? He had got enough money and was convinced that he would not be turned away.

The train was again quite empty when it arrived so he had the choice of where to sit. There wasn't a smokers carriage so he was free to sit wherever he liked. The young lad also got on the train but this time, sat quite a distance from him, but as he began to think about his own predicament, he did wonder if the other lad too, had decided to run away from home to seek his fame and fortune. What a coincidence, he thought. Soon the train pulled into Blackpool North station and everybody got off. He gathered up all of his luggage and proceeded to go through the barrier onto the main station concourse. There he would find a map.

He looked out of the glass doors of the railway station in the hope of seeing something from which he could take his bearings. He could clearly see the top of Blackpool Tower straight in front of him. He went back to the map. It may as well have been written in a foreign language for him. If he had got some idea of where to head for, then perhaps some sense could have been made from it. He began to scan the coastline and saw the Butlins Metropol Hotel clearly marked and thought that there must be guest houses in that area, so he decided to head for Talbot Road, in which he would turn left for the

sea. This he did. The road was quite busy so, he decided to turn off into a side road.

As he entered Cocker Street, he could see the sea ahead of him but was getting quite tired of carrying all of his luggage. Having noticed a hotel on the right advertising bed and breakfast for just ten pounds per night, he walked over to it. Quite expensive, he thought; but looking around at the notices on neighbouring buildings, all advertising at between ten and fifteen pounds for a nights stay, so he decided to go up the steps and then he rang the bell.

The door was answered by a large gentleman in his fifties who said that he did have a room available for one week and that if he wanted to stay for the week, it would only cost him fifty-five pounds. Having been given almost two hundred pounds in cash as presents, he knew that he could afford it, so he paid over his money and once registered, went up to his second floor room.

It was quite a nice room, compact but nice, He placed his bags by the dressing table and thought that he would wander down to the sea front. He was feeling hungry by this time and could smell hot dogs and onions being cooked somewhere. Two were purchased and then he wandered along the front. First towards the tower and then back towards his hotel. Yes, he thought; this is the place for him. He would set out in the morning to find work and once obtained, would look for somewhere more permanent to stay. He couldn't afford to pay the ten pounds per night for ever.

As he looked over to the sea, he noticed that there was a path leading down to the beach, and to some sort of concrete shelter. This needed further exploration, but still feeling quite tired, he sat down on a bench a mere matter of feet from the golden sands. Coming towards

him in the distance he could see the young lad who he had smiled at on the train. He was really too excited to speak so as the lad got nearer, he dropped his head so that eye contact would not be made. It didn't work. The young lad sat down on the other end of the bench but at first, didn't say anything. Damian glanced over towards him without moving his head and could clearly see a large bulge in his trousers. Looking at this soon had the same effect on Damian and it soon became clear that the other lad too, was keeping an eye on him.

"Been here long?" the lad asked.

"Only a few minutes."

"It'll get busier after ten. Should make a few bob then." Damian hadn't a clue what his new found friend was talking about. "I'm Tony by the way," he said offering his hand to Damian.

"I'm Damian."

"Nice name. I hate Tony. My real name's Anthony but everyone shortens it to Tony. I've got used to it now. Don't suppose yours does."

"Not really."

"Here on holiday?"

"No. I've left home."

"Blimey!" Tony exclaimed. "Mind you, I did that a couple of months ago. Down tools and everything. Bloody hard struggle though at first. Not so bad not that I'm known."

"Oh. You've made many friends then."

"Friends? I don't know if that's the right word. 'Clients' perhaps."

"Oh." Damian didn't realise what Tony was saying to him. To be honest he wasn't all that interested, although he did appreciate the opportunity of someone to be able to speak to.

"I saw you on the train but, I didn't want to speak."

"Why not? I would have spoke to you." Damian thought that this was quite strange. He could have spoken. Why would he not want to?

"You might have thought that I was trying to pick you up. I mean, I've never done it on a train before and the prospect would have excited me."

"Oh, I see." The penny finally began to drop. Not only was his new friend gay, but obviously what are referred to as rent boys. Damian had heard of such people but didn't have a true understanding of what the term really meant. Deep down Damian rather fancied Tony but dare not reveal that. He decided to keep the conversation fairly peripheral for that purpose.

"Is that why you kept going to the toilet?"

"It was really. The last time I knew that you were watching me so, I left the door unlocked, just in case."

"I'm sorry. I didn't realise. I'd got a lot on my mind really."

"Oh." Tony cheered up a little. Whilst he knew that Damian was gay, he had been wondering why the tender looking lad had not followed him into the train toilet. "I felt much the same when I left home. Thinking had I done the right thing and so on. It's not easy, especially for someone of your age."

"I'm sixteen. I know that I don't look it but I am. Today as it happens."

"Today? Crumbs. Been planning it for long?"

"Quite a few weeks. It's still a wrench though, even though you've sorted out everything in your mind. At least, I hope that I have."

"I know. I was nearly seventeen when I left. You got anywhere to live yet?"

"No. I'm staying at the hotel over there." Damian pointed to the sky blue neon lights around the front of the hotel. "It seems quite a nice place but I've not spent much time there yet. Do you know it?"

"Oh yes. 'Brian's Hotel' is well known around here for, well, how can I put it. It's one of Blackpool's more basic gay hotels."

"A gay hotel?"

"Yes. Didn't you know that?"

"No. I just walked down the road from the railway station, and perhaps it was the lights I don't know. I just seemed to be attracted to it. How do you mean it's a 'gay hotel'?"

"Boy! You've got to learn so much if you're going to go around of the scene. I mean, this things all right but, it is a bit risky."

"The scene?"

"OK. Let's go back to the beginning. I presume you're gay, and I don't know but perhaps due to persecution in the past, gays tend to keep themselves to themselves, and use certain pubs and clubs that straight people don't usually go to. It's called the 'scene' and in Blackpool and other places, some hotels that are run by gay people, specialise in attracting gay people to stay there. It's not that bad. Most of the places here are very good. You don't have to hide the fact that you're gay. You know?"

"Yeah. I had a few friends back home and I couldn't tell them that I wanted to have sex with them."

"Exactly and if you had, they would have taken the piss out of you something rotten. Your family would

find out, and that's when life goes all wrong. It did for me anyway."

Tony and Damian carried on talking for some time before Tony looked at his watch. His eyes strayed to the foreshore and the several pathways down to their location. It seemed as if they were the only people there. With the tide coming in the waves were beginning to lash the sea wall and they seemed totally oblivious to the fact that only a matter of a few yards behind them, the trams were running backwards and forwards, thundering across the bridge.

"You said that today was your birthday?"

"Yes. There's not much left of it now though."

"And are you sure that you've done the right thing?"

"Well, yes I suppose so."

"If you're not sure then, the best thing that you can do is to get back home. Fame and fortune doesn't come easily." Tony looked across at Damian whose face was beginning to look sad and dejected. "Well?"

"It's not that I don't want to be here, it's really a case of not knowing anyone and being in a totally strange place. That's all. I will get used to it and meet new friends, I know I will but it's quite strange just now." Tony moved next to Damian on the bench and put his arm around him. Damian was quite surprised about this and immediately looked all around him just in case other people might be able to see him.

"Cheer up." Tony could see that the bulge in Damian's jeans was as evident as his own, and slowly his other hand began to work its way up from Damian's right knee, onto his young crotch. Damian was surprised by this but made no attempt to push Tony's hand away. Instead, his right hand began to find its way to Tony's hot rod. "I

bet you wish now that you had followed me into the toilet on the train."

"Yes I do."

"You follow me," Tony said as he stood up; "and I'll make it a birthday that you'll never forget."

Tony began to walk down the concrete slope towards what looked like a couple of Victorian pillars and then seemed to disappear from view. Having first made sure that there was nobody about, he walked down that slope to find Tony. As he went between the pillars, he noticed that Tony was nowhere to be found, but some twenty yards along was a gents toilet and assumed that Tony had gone in there. He went in. It was dark and from the smell had not been cleaned for some time. As his eyes got used to the pitch blackness, he could just make out Tony's shape at one end of the toilet cubicles.

"This one's the biggest," Tony whispered as they both went in and the door was bolted from the inside. Damian felt Tony's hands removing his jeans and without warning, once his cock had been released from its sling, a warm mouth engulfed it in such a way that all Damian could do was to thrust backwards and forwards in rhythmic pleasure.

After a few minutes Tony stood up and removed his own jeans. Getting Damian to sit down, Tony moved nearer to him until he too felt a warm mouth upon his own throbbing tool. Just before exploding he withdrew and again went down on Damian and with one very well practised move, placed Damian's feet over his shoulder enabling him to enter the birthday boy. Once satisfaction had been achieved, both the boys got dressed and after arranging to meet the next day, Damian left the cubicle first and went over to wash his hands. Tony left the toilets.

As Damian turned he could see an older boy standing at the urinals. The boy could see Damian looking at him and pointed to the cubicle that had only just been vacated. Damian tried to explain that he had just finished but by this time, his jeans were around his ankles and he was bent over in a manner that could only mean one thing.

On his return to the hotel he was feeling very tired and although it was only ten past ten, he felt that he would just have time for a drink in the bar before going up to bed. As he nervously stood outside the hotel bar he heard a voice coming from upstairs.

"Hi. Enjoying your holiday?" Damian turned around. "Come on, I'll buy you a pint."

"Thanks."

"Don't worry. If you're staying here they'll serve you." Damian followed the lad into the bar. He couldn't have been much older than he was although, Damian looked much younger than his sixteen years. "I'm Steve. Lager?"

"Please. Damian." As he said this Steve looked at him.

"You don't have----------."

"No." Damian had heard that one so many times. Had he got three sixes tattooed on the top of his head. He thought that if he'd have got a pound for every time someone had said that to him then, he would by now be very rich.

He began to tell Steve all about himself and that he had run away from home. Steve didn't seem to be very surprised about this, recounting to Damian that he too had done the same thing some months ago, but now lived in Scarborough and was only here on holiday to celebrate his eighteenth birthday, which was on the following day.

"A lot of lads to run away from home. Well,

when I say run, I mean that they leave home at your age because their family wouldn't or couldn't cope with their sexuality. Coming out is not easy."

"Did you tell your parents?" Perhaps if Damian had told his parents then there would have been more understanding between them, and this by itself could have stopped him from running away.

"No. My dad died when I was only fourteen and at that age, well you don't really know who you are or which way you are going to go. Mum had guessed but I couldn't bring myself to tell her. She knows that I live with a guy and we have a one bedroomed flat, so if she can't put two and two together then I'm not going to tell her."

"I couldn't tell my parents or my brother. I think that he guessed and I think that although he's supposed to have a sort of 'girlfriend', he's really gay."

"And you?"

"Never had a girl and wouldn't know where to start but, I don't know that I'm gay."

"Have you had sex with boys?"

"Oh yeah. Dozens of times and I enjoyed it. Except with my brother."

"Blimey! You had sex with your brother. All the way?"

"Yes. Several times." Damian began to tell Steve about the times at home. That first time, when they shared a room, and his encounters in the park.

"And you don't know if you're gay?"

"No. Sexually I suppose that I am but, that's not all, surely."

"You're right it isn't. Sex is nice, it's good but, it's only about a third of any relationship - long term I mean. They all start off with nothing but sex but then, the

sex tends to calm down to once or twice a week. Here. Let me get you another drink."

The two boys carried on talking until gone midnight. Steve was intrigued and perhaps jealous that he had not had the same opportunities when he had been younger.

"Thanks for the drinks," Damian said; "but I'm so shagged out. I'll have a shower and hit the sack."

"I'm coming up myself now so, I'll show you where the shower is."

"Thanks."

Damian hadn't finished unpacking so he threw his bag off the bed, grabbed a towel and went off for his shower. As he came back to his room Steve was just coming out of his room, towel over his shoulder. They said goodnight and went their separate ways. As Steve returned from his shower, he noticed that Damian's door was still open and as he got nearer he could see him sitting on the corner of his bed, dressed only in his towel. He knocked on the open door. As Damian turned around, Steve could see the tears running down his childish face.

"Hey. What's up? Would you rather be alone?"

"No. Come in." Steve threw his clothes down on the floor and closed the door. He adjusted his own towel before sitting next to Damian on the bed. As Steve put his arm around him in an attempt to console him, Damian put his head on Steve's shoulder and cried. Steve was beginning to think that Damian was regretting leaving home but after ten minutes or so the sobbing stopped.

"Homesick?" Steve enquired.

"No. I was just thinking about all the friends that I've left behind and of the new ones that I've met." Steve was puzzled. "I think I'm starting to grow up."

Steve was still puzzled. "I know that it's right but it's just so daunting."

"You'll get there. It will just take a bit of time for everything to fall into place."

"I know. I'm sorry."

"You've got nothing to be sorry for. We all need to let go at times. Crying is natural. Don't worry about it. Here. Give me a cuddle." Damian began to cuddle Steve and again began to cry. Steve held him tight to himself and began to stroke his golden blond hair. Whether it was that or not he couldn't be sure but, he could feel Damian's hand on his towel and once opened, left no obstacle in Damian's path. Steve had never intended this and whispered to Damian, "you don't have to you know." With Damian saying that he wanted to, Steve decided to allow events to take their course.

Four

Damian woke the next morning feeling very sorry for himself. As he turned over Steve was still laying there. He began to feel very silly and embarrassed about the night before. He wasn't a cry-baby but, what did Steve really think? He began to feel even more embarrassed but got out of bed to make them both a cup of tea. The noise of the kettle boiling woke Steve. As he turned over to face Damian, he spoke.

"Morning," he said quickly moving over to Steve to kiss him. "Tea or coffee?"

"Tea. Morning. What time is it?"

"Ten to eight. What time do they serve breakfast?"

"Nine-thirty." Damian carried on making the tea and after placing it on the bedside table, jumped on top of the bed and Steve, kissing him again. Damian knelt up close to Steve so that there could be no question of what he wanted. As Steve raised his head from the pillow, Damian's cock - already hard - got its morning kiss. Once empty, Damian slipped the bedclothes down and impaled himself on Steve. Steve had never met anyone so rampant as his new found friend. It was one of the nicest gift-horses he had had for a long time.

Following a shower, breakfast. Both the lads were by this time ravenous and despite there being table numbers on each of the dining room tables, they decided to sit together in a corner of the room. It was all too evident that this was not just a chance meeting on the stairs but something more serious than that. Damian had been grateful for Steve's friendship, hence the novel early morning kiss but deep down.

Steve knew that the attraction shown by both to the other could only ever be peripheral, and purely a one off.   Much as he would have liked to allow their relationship to blossom and to bear fruit, he knew that he would have to go home in two days time, back to his boyfriend. He knew that Scarborough was just too far away to conduct an elicit relationship. He also knew that if he let the relationship continue, then Damian would be so upset when he left. The problem was that Damian just made him feel so good.

Steve was no stranger to Blackpool so perhaps foolishly, decided to take Damian on a tour of the tourist attractions. The tower, the pleasure beach, the three piers and so on. Indeed it was almost lunchtime before they came out of the tower and made their way to the North Pier.

"I'm knackered!" Damian exclaimed as they found somewhere to sit down between the almost continuous line of elderly people who had taken the opportunity of an early holiday break.

"Me too."   After five minutes or so of basking in the watery sun, Damian suggested that they went for a cup of coffee.   "You can get one on here but I know somewhere over the Promenade that serves real coffee, not the instant muck that you get in most places." Damian agreed and they set off along the Promenade until they saw a coffee bar that was conspicuous by the fact that it had the traditional 'Pride' flags flying outside. They went down the steps and Damian opened the door.

"Bloody hell!" he exclaimed.

"Sit down and I'll get the coffee."

What Damian hadn't been ready for was the fact that this was a gay coffee bar - the only one in Blackpool.   On the walls interspersed with posters

advertising the summer shows, were posters of scantily clad men and. details of several gay chat lines.

As he looked around the fourteen tables he began to realise that with one exception, each table was occupied by either two men or two women. He could hardly believe his eyes. This was the first of Blackpool's gay venues that he had visited other than his hotel, which had nothing like the display that he was now taking in quickly. When Steve came back to the table and their coffees' had been served he began to quiz Steve.

"What is this place?" he asked somewhat nervously.

"It's a gay coffee bar. It's run by gay people for gay people." Steve began to realise that all of this was new and strange to Damian. "Blackpool has got many places that are gay run and a lot that are for gay people only, or gay friendly.

"What does 'gay friendly' mean?"

"It means that gay people are welcome and that the place is usually patronised by gay people. If you don't like gay people and there are many people out there that don't, then they don't use such places. There's usually a warning outside, especially outside the pubs and bars, although most people know that they are gay venues and just leave them alone. Have you never been in one before?"

"No never. This is my first time."

"I like this place because you can be yourself. You don't have to hide away the fact that you're gay because so is everybody else. It's also somewhere where you can meet people and chat."

"Right. I see. And this is the only one in Blackpool?"

"It's the only one that's exclusively gay. There

are plenty more that are gay run but they don't cater just for the gay community. They can't afford to. They have to let anyone in."

"But not here?"

"No. I have only seen one couple who I didn't think were gay, but you never know they could have been. A lot of gay men enjoy the company of lesbians. Apart from that, if they're trying to hide their sexuality, then it appears as if they've got a girlfriend and they don't get any aggravation."

"Even though they've got a boyfriend at home."

"Yes. Get the picture?"

"I think so. I never knew that these places existed."

"They do. Anyway. Drink your coffee before it gets cold."

Steve just stared at Damian as he began to behave like a human sponge, soaking up the atmosphere and the novelty and wonderment of it all. It was just as if he had been in Wonderland with Alice and had joined her as she went through the door to the Mad Hatters tea party. The only difference now was that people seemed to be behaving rationally and not as if they had been playing without a full deck.

Just as they were about to leave, a young lad about eighteen came in with what looked like a dress in a dry cleaners polythene bag. Damian was rooted to his seat as the young lad spoke to the guy behind the counter to ask if he felt that it would be all right for the weekend. Steve too was surprised. Damien's' eyes were wide open with astonishment. He had heard of guys dressing up as women, but not ten feet away was one of them. It took Steve all his time to get Damian to get up and as they both left, Steve suggested that they went back to the hotel.

Once in the privacy of the hotel, this time Steve's room, he began to explain to Damian what it meant to be openly gay, and about the sort of characters that he was likely to come across. He felt too that the dangers ought to be spelled out.

"But if all gay people are so friendly, why should I worry?"

"There's a term used to describe very young gay people. They are called 'chickens' and I don't know of any gay person who would not given the opportunity, well and truly stuff one!"

"So?"

"Chicken describes boys between about thirteen and eighteen."

"Oh." Now, he could be classed as that. He wasn't sure whether he would like the term applied to him so, decided to let the matter go straight over his head.

Steve lay down on the bed and began to fall asleep. He hoped that he had done the right thing trying to explain to Damian all that he needed to know before he got himself into any real serious trouble. That's the last thing that he would want to happen but knew that because of his age, people would be so predatory towards him.

Damian was also feeling very tired. He sat on the edge of the bed looking down on Steve who by this time, had gently drifted off to sleep. He began to mull over in his mind what Steve had said to him. It was just as if he had been captured by aliens and transported onto another planet. In his wildest dreams, he never thought that life could be one endless round of shagging, sleep and then even more shagging. Wonderful! Yes, he had made the right decision to leave behind what he considered to be his dismal home life, and whilst he realised that the streets were not paved with gold, he knew that Blackpool was the

right place for him and, that he was right for it.

With all that had been going on that day he hadn't really been able to say to Steve that he had thought about coming out. Despite all of the reservations and the occasional feelings that he had had a couple of years ago for one of the girls at school, deep down he knew that he was gay. How would he convince others that he was. Would he need to? What would it really mean and how to do it. Questions he would ask Steve when he woke up. He knew that he wouldn't have to carry a large placard around with the words 'I'm Gay' on it but, perhaps because he so desperately needed to meet new people, he felt that the time was now right for him to 'come out'.

It was then that he remembered that today was Steve's eighteenth birthday and not only had he not wished him a 'happy birthday' when he presented him with breakfast in bed that morning, he had not even bought him a card or a present. Having made sure that Steve was sound asleep, he slowly and quietly crept out of the room. He remembered that there was a newsagents shop not that far from the hotel and, although he had no idea what to buy him, he could at least get him a card.

As he walked down the concrete steps of the hotel he glanced across to the sea. There seemed to be an unusual amount of people gathered almost opposite the road, so with his feline instincts aroused, he decided to find out what was going on. As he approached the crowd, he could see that they were all looking over the rails to the beach below. The tide was on its way out and as he looked over, he could see that what looked like a body had been washed up on the beach. This turned his delicate stomach and he knew that if he kept looking over then he would soon be sick. Fearing the worst, he made straight for the toilets where Tony had taken him on the day that

he had arrived. Seeking the first cubicle that was not engaged, entered and promptly threw up.

Some minutes later he realised that the wall of the cubicle had been defaced and that a large hole had been made in both side walls. He looked at the door and that too was not intact. Eventually curiosity got the better of him and he slowly leaned forward from his now seated position to look through the hole on his left. He realised that the cubicle was empty so with pulse racing, looked through the hole in the right hand wall. An eye was visible and he very quickly sat bolt upright. After three or four attempts the eye disappeared and he could see right into the cubicle. The light was then blocked and as he moved his face away. Whoever was next door inserted his cock into the hole so that it came straight through into Damian's domain. It took a few seconds before Damian held it tight and began to massage it gently, all the time struggling to keep his own in order. Relief given, the other man left.

Damian then turned his attention to the cubicle door and could see through to the urinals and those standing there. Most were old men in their fifties and sixties and they had never been a turn on for him, so having made the decision to deal with his own erection, he sat down. He then heard the door of the left had side cubicle close and again his curiosity got the better of him. It was quite a young boy, he thought, about fifteen and as he showed no interest in looking through at Damian, he thought that he would make his presence felt and put his own cock through the wall, just as the man had done to him. A warm mouth engulfed it for a minute or so and as he withdrew, the other boy did likewise. Damian sucked on it hard and after the boy withdrew, he heard him leave the cubicle. Then came a knock on the door. Damian opened it and the boy stood there. Taking absolutely no

notice of the other men in the toilets, went in so that they could continue together with a certain amount of privacy. Satisfaction both given and received, Damian knew that it wouldn't be long before Steve would be waking up so, remembering his real reason for his trip, he left.

Even though he hadn't known Steve for more than a day or so, he began to think of him as a close friend. Although he knew that the next day Steve would head back to Scarborough, he hoped that they would at least stay in touch and that perhaps Blackpool would again be visited by him. Oh how he wished that they could just live together and spend the rest of their lives together. Juvenile infatuation. Then he came down to earth with the reality that this would not be, and so he chose a card from the rack in the newsagents. As he walked back to the hotel he tried to think of something witty to write in the card before sneaking it into Steve's room.

As he sat in his own room desperately searching for the inspiration to write something that he hoped would be treasured, he thought of the good times that he and Steve had shared. A tear began to run down his face. Would he ever know happiness again? If not with Steve then, who with. If he was honest with himself, he hadn't thought that he would have met someone that quick. Oh, the sex was great. He had really enjoyed that but, he felt that perhaps after all, it was love that he had been desperately seeking. Just having someone there to cuddle you when the chips are down and, being able to repay the compliment. Then he remembered that Steve's boyfriend might see the card and thought that he had perhaps not write what he had been feeling and just add, 'love and best wishes from Damian' at the bottom of the card.

As he placed the card on Steve's bedside table, the object of his love began to stir.

"Oh Damian," Steve said as he noticed the card. "You're such a little treasure but you shouldn't have, really."

"But I wanted to. It is your eighteenth after all, and you're away from home."

"Come here and give me a cuddle." The two embraced. "What time is it?"

"Nearly three o'clock."

"Blimey! You should have woken me up."

"Like I did this morning?"

"No, not like that. Not that I didn't enjoy it, I did, but if I'm going to show you all the sights of Blackpool, then we had better get going. This is my last day."

"I know. I hope that the day never ends."

"Hey. Come on. I don't really want it to end and tonight I'm going to take you out to a pub that I know."

"But I'm only sixteen."

"Well, I know but even if you have to drink coke or something, I can always sort you out with a proper drink when we get back."

"OK."

The two lads got ready and went for a walk along the Promenade. Rock and presents were the order of Steve's shopping trip. They went into every arcade between the north and central piers looking for that special gift that Steve would need to take back to his partner.

"I always leave shopping until the last day. I hate it. Apart from that, I get so bored shopping, always have."

"I don't like it much either. Usually because I don't have enough money to buy what I want."

"Yeah. Tell me about it. Ah," Steve exclaimed

as they came across a small arcade by the Sea Life Centre. "You wait out here and I'll be back in a minute."

"Why?"

"Just wait there and I'll be back in a minute."

Damian stood outside the arcade looking at a stall selling tee-shirts. He couldn't understand why Steve insisted that he waited outside. It wasn't as if 'children' weren't allowed in because he could see through the open door that a lot of children were in there. It was a few minutes later when Steve finally came out.

"Did you get it?"

"Yes.   Sorry about that," he said quickly ensuring that his purchase was put to the bottom of the bag. "Come on. I'll take you for another coffee."

"Can we go back to that place we went to this morning? I quite liked that."

"Oh, you mean 'Axis'?"

"Yeah."

"Ok."

Damian was not quite so gobsmacked on his second visit but still sat there soaking up the atmosphere. There were a group of five lads about Steve's age sitting at one table at the back and a couple of older men sitting by the spiral staircase that led to a second floor. During their two hour visit people kept coming and going. He thought that it was quite a busy place. It was after Steve had bought their fifth cafetiere of coffee that he began to rummage through that afternoons purchases until he found a box about two inches wide by eight inches long. He had bought this last. As he fished it out of the bag he handed it to Damian.

"What's this?"

"Open it and see."   Damian couldn't get the wrapping paper off quick enough. As he opened the box

he could see a gold coloured neck chain. "Who's this for?"

"For you."

"But it's your birthday. You're supposed to receive presents, not give them."

"I know but, it's to say thank you for your company and other things."

"It's great."

"Here. Let me put it on for you." As he did so the tears began to roll down Damian's face. "Don't cry."

"No one has ever given me anything like this before."

"But you've made my birthday special and it's really to say thank you. It looks good too."

Damian stood up and looked in one of the mirrors. "Yes it does. Thank you." He wasn't going to leave it at that and reached over to Steve and gave him a long kiss on the lips. He didn't care now who was watching. Yes, he couldn't hide it anymore, he was out and proud.

Five

That night Steve kept his word and took Damian on what could only be described as a pub crawl. They started off at an underground bar called 'Linda's'. It was packed solid. There was only just enough room to squeeze into a fairly dark corner while Steve got the drinks. There was a disco blaring out music from the charts and some people - mainly guys - were trying to move about on the dance floor.

"Well, what do you think?"

"The music's quite loud, but it seems OK."

"You do get a lot of dykes in here. It's mixed."

"Mixed?"

"Yes. Guys and lesbians."

"Oh. Right."

Almost at the time that Steve had finished his drink, he noticed that Damian was getting strange looks from someone behind the bar. Fearing that it was because Damian was under age, Steve suggested that they leave quickly; which they did. As they walked up Talbot Road, Steve began to point out other things.

"You see that place over there with the dark blue neon light."

"Yeah."

"That's 'Phil's'. You don't get many lesbians in there but they've got a doorman on so we can't go in. It's smaller than 'Linda's' and you tend to get a lot of leather guys in there."

"Leather guys?"

"Yes. Guys who like to dress in leather."

"You mean bikers?"

"That sort of thing, yes. But they're not all

bikers. Some guys like to dress up like that. It turns them on."

"It wouldn't turn me on."

"Nor me.   Just leather?" he added after a moments thought.

"Just leather, socks and boots. Plenty of studs!"

"I don't think that I'll be going in there then. Especially if they have a doorman."

"Yeah. They won't let you in. Most places have doormen but 'Bodgers' only have doormen at the weekend. They'll let you in but you may have to drink coke. You'll have to dip your straw into my pint when no one's looking."

"Cheers."

"Up there," Steve said pointing towards the railway station; "is 'The Hanging Stiletto'. It's the latest gay pub and is next door to the gay night-club, 'Slingbacks'. You won't get in either of them."

"Right."

"From that point of view it's a pity that you don't look older but if you did, you'd probably spend all of your time in there, especially 'Slingbacks'. We'll walk past them on the way to 'Bodgers', then you can at least have a look from the outside."

"Why did they call it 'Bodgers'? It seems a silly name for a pub."

"Because, well you'll see when we get there. Just look at the place, its layout and its decor. I like the place because it's just like an ordinary pub and not an excuse for a club that pretends it's a pub like 'The Hanging Stiletto' does. I always feel very relaxed in there."

The two lads carried on walking for about half a mile before Steve pointed to the corner of two main roads.

"That's 'Bodgers' on the corner."

"It doesn't look much from the outside, does it."

"No but they're going to sort that over the winter and really make something of the place. I can't wait for it to be done out."

"Won't they have doormen here?"

"No. Only at weekends. They'll let you in all right, but you're probably going to end up with coke. I'll get you a straw!"

Damian couldn't believe his eyes as he went in. All of the wood panelling was dark mahogany and there were small areas of the pub all decorated differently. Now he realised why they had called it 'Bodgers'. Steve went up to the bar and Damian went down into the games room at the far end of the pub. There were guys about both their ages in there whereas, in the main part of the pub, there were couples of varying ages.

"Well," Steve asked. "What do you think of the place?"

"I don't know really. I've not been in many pubs before and this! It's something else."

"It's that all right. Don't be surprised if you see guys kissing each other. Where this place wins over the others on the scene is that it is run as a conventional pub. OK the couples are either both guys or lesbians and it has a disco and cabaret at the weekends but, that's the only difference."

The two boys sat down on a bench seat near the pool tables and began to chat. "The other thing that you're going to have to get used to is other guys looking at you."

"What do you mean?"

"Well, if two guys come in together, it is

assumed that they are an item."

"Item?"

"Yes. A couple. An affair. Guys will still look at you but they won't approach you."

"Approach me? What for?"

"God you're so bloody naive! For sex. They will look at you, then buy you a drink in the hope that you'll go back to their place and have sex, or they will follow you into the gents with the same purpose in mind."

"Right." Damian began to feel threatened. He could see that there were guys looking at both him and Steve and there was one guy in particular who every time his and Damian's eyes met, put his hand on his crotch as if to say; 'come and get it!'. "But if I was approached and said 'no', then they'd leave me alone wouldn't they."

"Not necessarily. Most would take the hint and look elsewhere, but after a couple of beers then, they can turn up the pressure. The thing to do is not to make eye contact. Ignore them and eventually they will get the message."

"But if I came in on my own-----"

"Then, you would be considered fair game. Looking around in here now, there's not one guy who wouldn't try to get into your knickers."

Damian felt flattered. Yes, he knew that he was attractive and had been picked up in the past, but this was a whole new ball game. He would be able to flirt and cock-tease. When he mentioned this to Steve, he carefully pointed out that it would not be a good idea. "If you do want to flirt because you fancy someone and are prepared to go all the way with them, then do it. If you're not prepared for that, don't."

The boys stayed for about two hours and as arranged between them, Damian used his straw to full

advantage, consuming large amounts of lager from Steve's glass. They played pool and darts and then Damian began to yawn and was getting very tired. So they left. On the way back to the hotel there were more questions to ask of Steve. All the answers began to fill Damian's head to the extent that he thought at one point that it would explode.

Once back in the hotel bar where they both enjoyed a full pint, Steve tried to make some order out of what he had been saying. He realised too that Damian had so much to learn, especially if he was going to be a 'scene person'.

"The scene everywhere is so predatory. Young boys like you are snapped up by guys who either only want you for sex - a nice arse ready for fucking - or to make money out of you by making you sell yourself for their evil profits. If you want my advice then, don't sleep with anyone until you know them better."

"I didn't know you all that well."

"That's different. I wasn't going to exploit you and to be honest, didn't really expect sex the first time."

"But I didn't know that."

"That's true. I only wish that I'd had someone older telling me about the scene and its pitfalls before I started going out."

"Why? Have you sold yourself?"

"No but, I did come very close to it." Steve told Damian about the situation that had developed when he was still sixteen and for some reason, didn't want Damian to fall into the same sort of trap. Deep down he knew that he was beginning to get very close to Damian and that the following day, he would have to leave to go back to Scarborough. He had no real intention of getting close, but he could feel that it was starting to happen. Steve knew that he must treat the situation as nothing more

than a holiday romance. A fling.

It was almost ten minutes to twelve when Steve realised just what the time was, and that he had not done any packing. Damian's offer of help was accepted and the two went upstairs to Steve's room. He opened his suitcases on the bed and gradually began to fold all of his clothes and filled the first case after including a carrier bag that he had brought for dirty washing. The second one couldn't be filled because of toiletries required for the morning. Steve moved the suitcase onto a chair.

"I don't really want to go," he said as he turned to face Damian who was sitting on the bed. "But I've got to. I've got to get back to work and all that." He looked Damian straight in the eye. "And I'll miss you more than anything."

"I'll miss you too." Damian laid down on the bed only to be joined by Steve. "Can I stay tonight, please?"

"I wouldn't have it any other way," Steve replied.

Very little sleep was had by either of the two boys who were both eager to fill each others body with their own, and equally to be filled by the other. About four o'clock in the morning, both finally drifted off to sleep.

The next morning Steve woke about eight and realising that he had to leave very soon, very quietly packed his case. He wrote a note for Damian who was still sleeping and then crept out of the hotel. How he wished that he could have stayed for just one more week, or that he had met Damian a week earlier. He knew though that if either had been a reality, that he wouldn't now be going back to Scarborough but making long term plans to stay in Blackpool.

As he sat on the train waiting for it to leave Blackpool North station he knew that if by some miracle Damian had wandered onto the platform, then it would take him all of his time to stay on the train. He knew that he had fallen in love with Damian. It was something that he had never meant to happen but, he recognised the symptoms for himself.

As he took one last look down the length of the platform, the train began to pull out of the station. At almost the same time, Damian opened his eyes, realised that Steve had gone and saw the note. He dressed and went back to his room, sat down on his bed and opened the envelope. Before he could read past the first three words, tears began to flood down his face.

"My Dearest Love. I didn't have the heart to wake you. Perhaps if I had done that, then things could have worked out between us. What we had was special and I shall never forget you. Forgive me but I couldn't say goodbye. Look after yourself. Love, Steve."

Damian brushed away the tears as the breakfast gong went. He washed his face to try to disguise the fact that he had been crying and went downstairs to the dining room. He couldn't sit at the table that he had shared with Steve, so he chose to take a table by the window and sat with his back to the others who were breakfasting.

As he ate and drank, he knew that he would have to put this experience behind him and carry on building his life. He would also have to look for somewhere to live, and for a job to pay for the necessities of life like food. Perhaps he should go back to 'Bodgers' and say 'yes' to the first person who offered him any form of affection. That thought was soon dismissed. Whilst drinking his third cup of black tea, he began to plan out his day. He would shower, change and then launch himself on

the unsuspecting world of Blackpool.

By lunchtime, he had managed to find the local Job Centre and went in to register as unemployed. He was handed a pile of forms to enable him to apply for every state benefit under the sun (or that was how it seemed to him); which he took back to the hotel and placed in the top drawer of the dressing table. Now for somewhere to live. That search was very unproductive. Everywhere that he tried, no one would take him seriously because of his age. Doors were almost closed in his face. He even tried the homeless advice bureau but they were of little help.

As he came out of there, he saw the Axis Coffee Bar so he thought that he would go in there. Then he remembered that there were a couple of flats advertised on the board. He hadn't been there very long when he noticed Tony coming down the stairs. He wasn't sure whether to speak or not, so he hid his face in a newspaper and pretended to read it. Tony ordered his coffee and had seen Damian so went and sat at his table.

"Hi," he said as he sat down.

"Tony."

"I didn't know that you knew about this place. It's only been open a couple of months."

"Yeah. Someone from the hotel told me about it. He brought me down yesterday."

"I see. Still enjoying Blackpool?"

"Yes. I signed on today."

"That's a start but where are you going to live?"

"That's the next problem. I can't stay in the hotel for much longer. Another week at the longest."

"There's a flat going next to me. It's only a one bedroomed place but it's quite big really."

"How much is it?"

"About £60 a week. Could you afford that?"

"I don't know how much I'll get otherwise I'd take it."

"If you're interested, you could always come to an arrangement with the landlord. It is fully furnished."

"Where is it?"

"Just round the back." Tony pointed to the back wall of the coffee bar.

"What next door?"

"No. About five minutes walk."

Damian began to think more and more about the flat that Tony continued to tell him about. He explained that he shared a two bedroomed flat with another lad but, that they were not an item. "We get on great together but each do our own thing. We're not tied to each other. There's nothing in it. Nothing between us."

"No. I didn't think that there was," Damian added. He thought that he may have offended Tony in some way, perhaps by implication. "Any chance of having a look at the flat?"

"Hang on. I'll go and ring the landlord now and fix up a time." Tony pulled a mobile telephone out of his pocket and began to dial the number as he went outside, either for privacy or to get better reception. Damian thought that he had been talking for several minutes when Tony came back in. "Three o'clock today," he said as he came back to the table.

"Great." Damian thought for a moment. "I'll get you another cup of coffee. That one's gone cold."

Damian could hardly believe his luck. The possibility of getting a flat next door to someone he knew. Then he thought. His luck could never in a million years be that good, but he would go along to see the flat anyway. What he was unsure about was when Tony had mentioned that he 'could always come to an arrangement with the

landlord'. His suspicions subsided as the two lads talked about the video that was being shown on the four television screens dotted about the bar. They stayed until fifteen minutes to three and then Tony took Damian to view the flat.

As they approached the building, Tony pointed out his lounge window and said that the one on the far side, belonged to the vacant flat. Damian was quite surprised that the building was as big as it was, looking like two houses had been joined together. In the event, that had been the case. They walked over the recently tarmaced drive and in through the main door. As they entered, Tony explained that there were five flats in the building and that the landlord had the one at the back on the ground floor. He rang the landlord's bell and shortly afterwards the landlord emerged and gave Tony a set of keys.

The two lads went upstairs and Tony opened the door to the vacant flat. As he did so, the smell of stale air rushed out.

"It stinks a bit but that's only because it's been shut up for a long time. Mine was the same." Damian was quite surprised by how well the place was furnished. Although not sure what to expect, he had had visions of threadbare carpet - if any, a sink and small electric cooker in the kitchen, a bedroom similar to that of the hotel, and a lounge too small for a mouse to be swung around in.

As it happened the flat appeared palatial with plenty of cupboard space in all rooms. The bathroom had both a shower and bath in addition to the usual plumbing and, was carpeted. "All you need are your clothes and personal bits."

"I like it. It's got a very homely feel to it," he added bouncing up and down on the bed. "And it's only

£60 a week?"

"Well, mine's sixty but that's two bedroomed. You may get this for £50. I'll go and have a word with the landlord." Tony left Damian to have a good look around. The flat put his hotel room to shame, but how was he going to afford £50 each week. About ten minutes later Tony came back.

"Well?"

"I've spoken to Keith and he will let the flat go for £50 but that doesn't include bills."

"Bills?"

"Yeah. You know, gas electricity and water."

"Right. Mind you I shan't use much of that."

"Keith's happy that your DSS and apart from a deposit, he's happy to wait until your benefit is sorted."

"How much deposit?"

"One hundred pounds."

"That'll leave me pretty well skint." He knew that the chance of anything else coming up in the not too distant future would be remote so, he would have to think quickly.

"Come and have a look at mine." Tony showed Damian around his flat which again was quite plush. Almost as plush as his own home and he knew that it cost his parents much more than £60 a week for that. As the lads went back into the empty flat, Damian knew that he had to make his mind up there and then.

"I'll take it."

"Come down and meet Keith and I'll leave the two of you to sort it all out. Come back up when you've finished."

"OK."

Tony took Damian back downstairs to meet the landlord. Keith was a guy in his late thirties and fairly

well built.   He invited Damian in and they began to discuss the tenancy. Damian was really too excited to take in everything that Keith was telling him but kept nodding and agreeing at the appropriate gaps in the conversation.

"With you, I'll have six boys here so I don't want any falling out. You either get on with the other lads or you don't. Either way, I don't want any trouble. Keep yourself and the flat clean and there won't be any problems."

As he said that Damian began to look around at the pictures on the walls. Most were of naked young boys of about his age. Damian presumed that his landlord was also gay but at that time, thought no more about it.

"Your new to Blackpool then."

"Yes."

"And you're staying in a hotel?"

"Yes."

"So, you could say that I've done you a favour in renting you the flat."

"Yes."

"OK. Just sign the paperwork then we'll see if you can repay the favour in some way."

Damian signed the tenancy agreement, said that he would pay the money the next day and then move in. He was so full of excitement and felt that if he chose to contact his parents again, at least he could say that he had his own place and, that it was nice.

"You haven't seen my flat have you. This is the kitchen, the bathroom and in here is the bedroom." Keith closed the bedroom door behind them. "What about doing me a favour. Kneel down and enjoy!"

Six

Damian collected the keys to the flat and made his way back to the hotel. He told the owners that he would be moving out the next day and collected the money that he had paid in advance. They charged him for an extra day for the inconvenience but he was still on too much of a high to realise that he could really have left there and then. He showered and changed ready to unleash himself upon the people of Blackpool.

Even though Steve had during their brief time together shown him around the scene and had taken him along to the Job Centre, he knew that he would have to start there in order to get a job. As he walked in, the young lady on reception remembered him and he gave her his change of address.

On his way out he decided to look on the notice boards to see if there were any vacancies that might interest him. There were several jobs that he thought that he might do, but as he read further down the particulars of the vacancies, it became clear that he did not have the experience to be able to carry them out. He became very despondent and by this time was feeling very hungry. He decided that he would make his way to the Axis Coffee Bar for a sandwich to keep him going until later that day.

Damian suddenly came back to earth with a bang. He knew that the rent for his flat would be paid whilst he remained unemployed and once the council offices opened the next morning, he would go down and make his claim. The unemployment benefit that he would get would pay the bills but that it wouldn't leave much money for life's essentials. He still had a couple of hundred pounds but that would go in no time and it would

be at least a couple of weeks before a giro landed on his doorstep. Work would have to be his next priority.

As he sat there drinking the last drop of coffee, he looked through one of the gay newspapers that were on the table, obviously left by the previous incumbent. He could overhear part of a conversation between a couple of guys on the next table talking about a place called 'Central Walk,' and the fact that it wasn't all that far away from the coffee bar. The words; 'I'll pick one up for twenty' came across quite strong but Damian had no real idea what the two men were talking about.

He tried to listen in to their conversation but their voices seemed to get quieter. He decided that a call of nature was required and passed their table. One of the men smiled and Damian returned the smile. On his way back however, he noticed that they were whispering.

Damian knew that they were talking about him. As he got back to his table he continued to read the newspaper but from the corner of his eye, he could see both the men looking at him. He took no notice of them and pretended to ignore them, knowing full well why. The two men were in their forties and were looking at him in such a way that he knew that they wanted him, between the sheets. He could see that one of them had an erection but having recently been emptied of his juices, there was no response from his own body. He decided to pay for his sandwich and coffee and left.

It was almost seven o'clock so Damian went back again to the hotel. This time he ensured that all of his possessions were carefully packed ready for the following day. He would breakfast and then go round to his flat, unpack and then look for work. By eight o'clock he was bored. It was too early to sit in the hotel bar and he didn't want to visit any of the gay bars. Instead he

walked down to the North Pier and sat down on one of the benches.

He sat gazing out to the sea whose tide was just going out. The noise of the waves splashing around the pier were masked by the noise coming from one of the bars, so he decided to move further along the promenade and to the other side of the Metropol Hotel. This was where he had met Tony on his first night.

Instead of sitting down on one of the benches, he decided to stop by the rails so that he could look right down on the waves below. After a few minutes he could hear the footsteps of someone coming up behind him and very soon, one of the men who had been in the coffee bar stood some six feet away to his right.

"Twenty," the man said just so that Damian could hear. He didn't react and chose to ignore the man. "You won't get any more." Damian still stood there taking no notice of the man. "Come on;" the man added. "Twenty quid for a blow job." Damian turned his head to face the man. He had assumed that he was talking to him but wanted to be sure. "Yes?"

"Were you talking to me?"

"Yeah. Twenty quid for a blow job."

"Where?"

"Down there in Central Walk." Ah. So this was Central Walk. The pennies began to drop. This was the place that they were talking about earlier. Damian looked at the man and nodded. The man gave Damian a twenty pound note and followed him into the toilets. Ten minutes later, he was back watching the waves. A thought occurred to him that perhaps he wouldn't need to find a job. If he could earn that sort of money every night then, why would he need to work. Twenty pounds and he didn't even have to take his clothes off. What an incentive! He

decided to sit down on the bench. As he did so, he saw Tony walking towards him.

"Hi. How did you get on with Keith?"

"OK. I move in tomorrow."

"Great. At least I'll have someone to talk to if Tom is out."

"Yeah."

"But how did you really get on with Keith?"

"What do you mean? He seems a nice enough guy." Tony sat down.

"I didn't mean that. Did you cop off?"

"Oh. You mean did we have sex? Oh yes. He was so gentle as well."

"He always is. You might find yourself down there a lot. He's into chicken."

Now where had he heard that expression before? It was the first time that he and Steve had gone into the coffee bar. Damian's curiosity got the better of him.

"How do you get on with him?"

"Me?" Tony hadn't prepared himself for the question to be fired at him. "Fine." He looked across at Damian who was obviously waiting for the whole story. "He's had us all. It's part of the deal. If we've got no trade, we usually end up down there - sometimes all of us - and well, it does pay the rent."

Damian had been very apprehensive when he had first entered Keith's flat but hadn't realised until now that it could be a regular thing, or that it was part of the deal of renting the flat. He thought that with six boys there that their landlord would be knackered if he had one of them every night.

"Are you looking for trade," Tony said; "or just admiring the view?"

"The view really although, this guy came up to me and offered me twenty quid to give him a blow job."

"Did you?"

"Yes."

"Then you're here for trade, not the view. It's all right there is plenty to go around. We charge twenty for a blow job given, thirty for a blow job received; after all you've got to get the juices back quickly. Forty if they want screwing and fifty if they want you to bend over."

"Blimey!" Damian sat back on the bench. "So," by this time he had realised that it was the money that had brought Tony out; "how much can you make in a night?"

"About a hundred. Some nights are quieter than others and if you've just cum then, it's about two hours before you're ready again, so you can't always give it. Mind you, if I'm not very keen on the guy then I fake it."

"You fake it?"

"Yeah. If you've got your dick up them, they don't know that you ain't shot, so you give them all the noises and get out of there quickly. Let's face it, you've got the money so why worry, especially if you really fuck them hard at the end."

"Right."

"The only problem is that you've got to let yourself go soft. If you're still hard they could guess that you've faked."

"I'll remember that."

"Here's one of my regulars so, I'll see you later."

Tony walked off into the distance. Damian really began to think. He could see his body. There would be more than enough people wanting it, but the

figures that Tony had told him about charging just seemed like telephone numbers to him.

He had earned money this way before but didn't really do it for the money then. It was the pleasure that he endured that in his mind was the priority. He couldn't remember ever faking it before, but did recall that sometimes it did take him much longer to explode that fountain of youth for his partner of the time.

He couldn't settle. The excitement of moving into his own flat kept him bubbling away inside. Would he keep the settee where he had seen it or should he perhaps reorganise the room. He drifted off into a world of his own and hadn't realised that a young lad of about nineteen had sat down on the other end of the bench. Without saying a word, the lad gradually moved closer and closer to Damian until there was barely a foot between them.

"How much?" the lad asked quietly. Damian did not reply. He was too deeply in thought. "How much?"

"Sorry," he said coming back to the present. "What for?"

"All the way."

"Forty." Damian had still not really been listening properly.

"I ain't got that much. I'll give you twenty."

"OK. Where?"

"I've got a place just over the way."

Damian agreed to go with the lad and they crossed over the road, walked past the hotel that Damian was staying at, around the corner and up three flights of stairs. The lad fumbled for his keys and eventually opened the door to a very dingy bedsit. They both went in.

"Fancy a coffee?"

"Please. I'm Damian. One sugar."

"Gary. I've not seen you about there before."

"No. I've only recently arrived. Mind if I smoke?"

"No. Have one of these." Gary threw a packet of cigarettes which landed on the couch next to Damian. He lit two and handed one to Gary in exchange for the coffee. "How old are you?"

"Sixteen. You?"

"Nineteen. I started like you. Most of us do. We run away or leave home and end up on the game. I've got my own punters so, it pays me enough to bring lads like you back here."

"I ran away too."

"I can tell. It's easy really. Those who have just come up on holiday act differently that the guys who live here, especially if they're your age."

"How can you tell?"

"They keep moving about. They don't sit and wait just in case they're seen by their family. If they are spotted then, it looks as if they're just walking along the prom."

"Oh."

"You don't look sixteen," Gary said looking deep into Damian's eyes. "You're a real babe." They kissed and Gary gently led Damian into the bedroom, first making sure that their cigarettes had been extinguished.

The room was dark with deep red wallpaper. Gary got undressed first and then insisted that he removed every item of Damien's clothing himself. Once both the boys were naked, they kissed again and Damian fell backwards onto the bed. Gary carefully caressed Damian until he reached the top of his pubic hair. He kissed his

navel and then went down on Damian ensuring that the erection was one that he wouldn't forget. Damian moaned with pleasure as he was almost brought to climax. Gary sensing this slowly turned him over and after gently massaging that eager hole, ploughed his own nine inches straight in.

After both had reached satisfaction, Gary lay next to Damian. Gary felt a hand quickly bringing him back into life and this time allowed Damian to enjoy himself quickly exploding inside Gary. The boys showered and dressed. After another cup of coffee, Damian left the flat and made his way back to the bench where he had been picked up from. There was no intention in his mind of more sex that night but after what seemed to be no more than half an hour, he was approached again. This time it was by three lads who were in their early twenties.

"We'll go down there," one of the lads said pointing to an area past the toilets.

"Yeah," another one of them added.

Damian began to feel frightened, especially when one of the lads got hold of him quite firmly. They walked down past the toilets and then took a path that led them down to the sea. It was very dark and there was no one about. At first there seemed nothing for Damian to worry about as the oldest lad undid his trousers and pushed his cock into Damian's mouth. The others stood there laughing and whispering to each other.

One lad seemed to be pointing towards a small opening in the wall, a sort of cave and Damian was taken there and stripped. He felt something around his wrists and realised that he had been tied to the wall.

By now, fear began to fill Damian. A handkerchief was pushed into his mouth and cock after

cock was pushed into his arse for the lads pleasure. One
of the lads laid down and Damian was released so that he
could sit on the vertical cock. Once that was inside him he
was bent over and another was pushed into him. The pain
was tremendous and he began to cry.   The gag was
removed at the same time that his balls were held very
tight so that he would not cry out as again, meat was
provided for him to suck on.

Once the boys had left, Damian got dressed but
waited for about ten minutes before leaving. He wouldn't
wait around for more but made straight back to the hotel.
Once in the comparative safety of his room he burst into
tears.

For the first time since leaving home, be began
to wish that he hadn't moved away. Yes, he had been so
full of confidence when he had slipped out of the house
and boarded the train to Blackpool, but he now realised
just how foolish that he had been. He decided to shower
and by the time that he had returned to his room, all
thoughts of home had vanished. The boys had paid him
well for his services but as he looked down at the sixty
pounds laying on the corner of the dressing table, he knew
only too well that he must not rely on selling his body for
his income, but that he must get a job. With determination
in his heart he slept. Tomorrow was to be a busy day.

In the morning he woke just before the
breakfast gong sounded. He looked at his watch and
realised that he had slept through and that if he wanted his
breakfast, then he would have to get a move on.   He
quickly dressed and went down to the dining room.   He
chose a table by the window which meant that he would
have his back to the other residents. He couldn't wait to
leave. The hotel was quite nice, but there was nothing like
your own front door which, he would have in less than an

hour's time. There he could do as he liked and would only have himself to please. A selfish thought, but why not.

Having breakfasted, he went up to his room to pack the remaining items before checking out. As he turned the corner of the landing, he noticed that the neighbouring bedroom door was open and with feline instincts taking over again, decided to peer round the door.

"Hi," a voice said. "Come in." Damian entered the room. There was a young lad drying himself after showering in his en suite facility and as he turned around, Damian felt that he knew the lad that was standing there. He was much older in his twenties. "Close the door." Damian did so.

"I can always come back later," Damian said, not wishing for the lad to be embarrassed.

"No please stay." By now the lad had finished drying but didn't bother getting dressed. He just lay on the bed so that Damian's eyes could only rest on one place. "Sit down." Damian sat on the corner of the bed. "I'm sorry," the lad said as he held Damian's arm. "About last night. We were all pissed."

Damian stood up ready to leave the room. He realised that the lad next to him was one that had almost raped him the night before. "You didn't get your fun," he added thrusting a twenty pound note into Damien's shirt pocket. "Here."

The lad quickly parted Damian from his jeans and began to give him head. As his erection gathered momentum the lad's position changed revealing an eager hole which Damian filled, giving the lad the roughest ride that he could. He wasn't frightened this time because there was only one of them, and he could see everything that was going on. He made sure that if the situation turned nasty, then he would be able to pick up the table

lamp and to do some damage with it.

There was no need. The lad was so gentle with him that the anger that was building up inside Damian began to subside. If it hadn't been quite an attraction to the lad, Damian would never had entered the bedroom in the first place, once of course that his curiosity had been eased.

Some ten minutes later Damian left the room and went to his own room, firmly locking the door behind him. 'Revenge is sweet', he thought and as he carefully put the twenty pound note into his wallet, he collected up his bags and left the hotel.

Damian walked down the road to the Promenade, along for about five minutes until he could see the Imperial Hotel in the distance. He turned right and headed for the small road that dissected his journey and walked up to the house which contained his flat.

The nervously felt for the bunch of keys that Keith had given him, and opened the outer door. He began to climb the stairs, slowly at first and then two at a time until, he reached his goal. His own front door. Standing outside the door felt strange at first and then with a very broad smile, put the key in the lock and opened the door.

He placed his bags down on the settee and then went back to close the door, stopping only to ensure that the kettle was full and beginning to boil. There was a small hook just inside the kitchen and it was there that he found home for his keys. He must remember that they were there and to take them every time that he went out. Keith would always have a spare set just in case he locked himself out, but he didn't want to appear a complete idiot by locking himself out. He remembered doing it at home and getting bollocking after bollocking for doing so. This

would not happen here.

He went through the flat opening all of the curtains and a couple of the windows in order to get some light and fresh air into the place. Kettle boiled, he sat down in an armchair, drank his tea and then proceeded to unpack.

Yes. This was now his home.

Seven

Damian spent the next two days in his flat only venturing out to buy food and the odd newspaper, cigarettes or milk. There were no trips to Central Walk or to any of the towns gay venues. Into the corner shop and back home again. For the first time in his life, he felt free. There were no constraints upon him. No house rules that he had to obey. Free to come and go as he pleased, to do what he liked, when he liked, with whoever he liked, and for that matter, how he liked. He also felt safe and that was now very important for him. Letter writing was not one of Damian's strong points, but he had managed to write to Steve, making sure that his new address was on the top of the letter. How he hoped and prayed for a reply. Postcards had been sent to his friend Jason, and for the first time since leaving home, a postcard to his parents, just to say that he was all right; without giving them his new address or any contact telephone number.

Housework was something that Damian had never much bothered with but now, he was quite happy to parade up and down, taking the vacuum cleaner over the carpets and to make use of the can of spray polish that he had found in one of the kitchen cupboards. He had only just finished reorganising the lounge furniture when his door bell rang. Visitors. As nobody knew where he lived, he was a bit curious as to who would be calling upon him at eleven o'clock in the morning. As he opened the door, Tony stood there.

"Hi," he said as the door opened.

"Tony. Come in. You're my first visitor!"

"Great," Tony added as he sat down on the settee. "Just popped round to say sorry for last night."

"What about last night?"

"Oh. I brought a guy back and we were making a bit of noise. Half thought that you'd have your ear to the wall."

"No. I went to bed about tenish. Was it worth it?"

"He paid well but wanted to cover me in baby oil before we got down to it and because we couldn't get a grip of each other we just kept on laughing."

"I didn't hear a thing, honestly."

"You're such an angel! You ought to try it sometime. I don't really find it a turn on but it does make a change from just getting down to it."

"I might, you never know. If the opportunity ever presents itself to me. Coffee?"

"Please"

Damian went off into the kitchen to make the coffee. No he hadn't heard anything the night before but if he had, well. Perhaps an ear will find its way to the wall on future nights. He would make a note of that and remember that if he did hear anything one of these nights, just to grab a brief listen.

The two boys carried on talking for almost an hour before Tony left. Washing had to be done and the invitation for Damian to call next door for coffee was made. Damian said that he would call one morning but not too early. He said that he was unsure of his plans but would definitely call. Damian tidied away the mugs that they had been using, emptied the ash tray and gave it a quick rinse under the tap before drying it and putting it back in the middle of the coffee table.

He was quite pleased that Tony had called because the novelty value of having his own place and sharing his own company was beginning by now to wear

off a little. The previous night although he had gone to bed early about ten o'clock, he had felt just a little lonely as he watched television beforehand. He realised that part of the boredom that was beginning to set in was because he would now be at home all day and not out at work. He knew deep down that this was going to be the hardest obstacle that would have to be overcome and, overcome quickly if he was going to be able to survive. He looked in the kitchen cupboards and realised that the food stock that had been there on his arrival was almost down to nothing and that he would need to go a substantial shopping trip quite soon.

'There was no time like the present', he thought so after checking that he had enough money on him and that he was appropriately dressed, decided that he would go down to the local supermarket and restock both the fridge and cupboards that were now almost bare. This would be quite an experience and expensive.

He knew how to boil things, open tins, fry things and toast bread but had never really had to do anything else in the kitchen before. The knowledge to be able to successfully cook a three course meal had not been learned, but would now have to be. All this to be borne in mind as he carefully locked the flat door and made his way down the staircase, and into the street.

The supermarket wasn't all that far from his flat so he wouldn't have to carry his purchases too far on the return journey. The first obstacle was to secure a shopping trolley and if he could, find one that had at least three wheels going in the same direction. Thinking that it would be a good start, began to shop.

About three-quarters of the way round, he met one of the guys that he had seen in the Axis coffee bar. They chatted briefly and then both went on their way.

Damian's trolley was quite full as he approached the checkout, only to be beaten by Andrew.

"We meet again," he said as he saw Damian behind him in the queue.

"Yes. Small world!"

"We've run out of fresh stuff so I've been sent out. I hate shopping."

"I'm just getting used to it. I'm not mad keen though. Could always find something better to do."

"Yeah. Are you coming in later?"

"Probably."

"I'll catch you later then." Andrew paid for the green-grocery and bread that he had bought and Damian began to empty his trolley onto the conveyor belt. He stood watching as the goods moved nearer to the scanner and could help thinking to himself; 'set of glasses, rotisserie, cuddly toy'; and at one point almost laughed. He paid for his goods, almost sixty pounds worth, packed them into seven large carrier bags and began the walk home after retrieving his £1 coin deposit on the trolley.

As he passed the entrance to the car park that was integral to the store, the noise of a car horn caused him to turn around. It was Andrew.

"Can I give you a lift?"

"Please." Damian piled the carrier bags onto the back seat of the car, got in and within two minutes was home. "Thanks," he said as he got out of the car. "See you later." Andrew drove off and Damian took the bags into his flat and unpacked. That was the worst part of shopping, the putting away when you got home.

Each time that he had gone down to the Axis coffee bar, Damian had been quite apprehensive. It hadn't stopped him going, but with it being obvious from the outside that it was a gay coffee bar, he had wondered who

had seen him go down the steps. On this occasion he had no such apprehension. Perhaps it was because he had spoken to Andrew in the supermarket or whether it was because he had been there several times, he wasn't sure. But he did note that perhaps for the first time, that he just couldn't give a damn who saw him. He could at least now lock himself away from the world and everybody in it if he wished to. Privacy, solitude, sanctuary.

"Hi Andrew," he said as he closed the inner door.

"Hi. Grab a seat and I'll be with you shortly. David's had to go out so I'm on my own for a couple of hours."

"Need any help?"

"Well, you're welcome to clear a few tables if you don't mind."

"No, I don't mind."

Damian began to gather up the dirty crockery off six of the tables and took it into the kitchen. Almost without thinking he grabbed the container of cleaner and a cloth, proceeding to wipe all of the tables down and to empty the ash trays as he went. Andrew brought him over a cafetiere of coffee and over the next hour or so, every time a table was vacated, Damian quickly and without being asked, cleared away the crockery and wiped the tables down.

When it quietened down, Andrew brought over another cafetiere and the two began to chat. Part way through the conversation Andrew thanked Damian for his hard work.

"You can have that on us for helping out."

"Are you sure? I didn't do it for that."

"No. I realise that but I appreciate the help. Things are getting much busier now than when we first

opened."

"That's good."

"It is but, when I'm in the kitchen and I can be for four or five hours constantly, there's only David or Sam out here and it's a struggle to keep all of the tables clear and to get the washing up done. In fact, we've been talking about getting someone in just to do that."

"Full time?"

"Not at first, perhaps eleven to six. At least then if we're not that busy, we can get on with the paperwork or those nasty tasks that go with running a business."

"Anyone in mind?"

"Not really. We do have someone who bails us out when we need a day off for something but she wouldn't work those hours for the money that we could afford to pay someone."

"Oh." Damien's' eyes fell. Andrew noticed this but at first couldn't understand it. "Would I do?" he asked quietly. "I would work hard, and I do need a job."

"I hadn't thought about you because I thought that you were just here on holiday, but if you're interested, I'll speak to Dave and Sam and get back to you."

"Great!" He face lit up.

"No promises mind."

"Oh no. I realise that, but I am looking for a job and would work hard." Andrew ran his fingers through Damien's hair and smiled. "Thank you."

This would be a dream come true. He hadn't really envisaged himself cleaning tables and washing up for a living, but he did remember when he looked through the vacancy boards in the jobcentre that there did seem to be quite a lot of them and with it being a seaside town, there was the strongest likelihood that he would end up in

the catering industry somewhere. Perhaps he would even pick up a few tips on cookery so that he would be able to look after himself at home. That would be heaven.

As he sat drinking his coffee he began to plan out his day, sure in his own mind that the job would be his. It would also give him an opportunity to meet people, to chat about this and that instead of risking going into the gay pubs where not only he was, but looked well under age. Shortly after the conversation with Andrew, David came back and the two of them went into the kitchen. Damian could only hear murmurs of the conversation but did hear his name mentioned on a couple of occasions. David came out, looked across at Damian and then went back into the kitchen.

Damian was feeling quite embarrassed by this time, so he felt that it might be better if he left and then came back later. He went up to the counter to pay but Andrew insisted that both his drinks were on the house because of the help that he had given. Damian insisted on paying for one of them and said to Andrew that he would be back later. Andrew winked at Damian as he went out of the door and up the stone steps to the pavement.

What would he do now? He didn't really want to go back to the flat because he knew that all he would do would be to pace up and down until he knew whether or not the job at Axis would be his. Neither did he want to just walk the streets, so he decided that he would walk down to the North Pier and catch some of the summer sun.

As he looked over onto the beach, he could see people swimming in the sea. From his vantage point the sea did indeed look appetising, but further out it was a dark brown colour that put paid to any idea that he had of joining them. He remembered then that there was a public pool not far from his flat. Taking the bull by the horns, he

did no more than walked home, collected his bathing trunks and a towel before heading off to the baths.

How fortunate that he had packed them in the rush before leaving home. He hadn't done so deliberately, they just must have got swept into his bag when his knickers and sock draws were being emptied.

Although not a very strong swimmer, other than snooker it was the only sport that he enjoyed. House swimming at school was really a mess about in the water rather than going up and down the pool to strengthen his stroke, but he thought that perhaps an hour or so would not only do him some good but would also help to take his mind off the possibility of getting a job at Axis.

After half an hour or so in the pool, he noticed that there was another boy who looked about the same age as himself. Although Damian was trying to swim lengths of the pool rather than just having a splash around, it seemed that the young boy was following him. He smiled at the boy who returned his smile but then carried on with his swim. It was about an hour later when he finally decided that he had done his stint for the day and got out of the pool. Damian dried himself carefully and changed back into his sweatshirt and jeans. It was when he took his trainers out of his locker that he noticed the young boy also changing. Again smiles passed.

Damian began to walk back to his flat to take his wet towel and trunks home and it wasn't until he turned the bottom corner of the road that he realised that the young boy seemed to be following him. He thought that perhaps the boy lived locally so again, didn't pay too much attention to him. Indeed, it wasn't until he had got to his flat and was putting his wet things into the washing machine that he noticed through the kitchen window that the boy was standing on the opposite side of the road, just

looking up at the flat. This he found very odd. Perhaps he had his own stalker and hadn't realised it.

As he straightened up the net curtain in the lounge he could still see the boy, and once he had made the decision to deliberately look out, the young boy immediately saw him and waved. He wondered then if it was someone that he already knew but couldn't place the face. Then he saw the boy cross the road as if he was coming into the block. Damian was by now even more confused. He went to his flat door and opened it. As he looked down the stairs, he could see the boys head showing through the glass panel of the downstairs door. He decided to go down to find out what the boy wanted.

"Hello," Damian said half opening the front door.

"Hello," the young boy said.

"Can I help you?" Not an original line but Damian just didn't know what to say. Perhaps he was a friend of one of the neighbours or looking for the previous occupant of the flat.

"I saw you at the pool."

"You'd better come in." Against his better judgement, Damian allowed the boy into the building and into his flat. "I'll make you a coffee."

"Thanks. Milk and one sugar please."

"Sit down. I think you've got some explaining to do."

"Oh." The boy sat down on the settee and waited for Damian to bring through the coffee. "I don't know if I should've come."

"Why did you?"

"I saw you at the baths and you just seemed to be a very nice person."

"Is that why you followed me home?"

"Yes." The boy was by now very close to tears and Damian sensed this. "Perhaps I shouldn't have."

"Drink your coffee."

Damian realised that the boy was in a certain amount of distress. Why, he had no idea but having got himself into this situation, needed to get out of it one way or another. The boy asked if he could use the facilities and Damian directed him to the smallest room.

"You've got a nice place here."

"Thanks. It's only rented. I've not been here long but I'm getting it the way that I want it. I'm Damian."

"Danny. Perhaps I shouldn't have come. I'm being silly."

"No you're not. Do you live around here?"

"Yeah. At the home round the corner. It's all right, but there's twenty of us there and it's a bit cramped."

"No privacy. Being told what to do all the time. I had that at home. That's why I moved." For no apparent reason Danny began to cry. Damian began to console Danny and put his arm around him. It was then that he noticed that his young friend had forgotten to do himself up after his call of nature. Damian could just make out a line of pubic hair through the gap in his trousers. His new found friend obviously choosing not to wear anything underneath them. He would say something about it before Danny left. He did glance down at his own fly, just in case.

Danny began to tell Damian about the children's' home and that he had been abused by some of the older boys. It turned out that Danny was only fourteen, which made Damian take a much longer look at that line of pubic hair which was now clearly visible to

him. It appeared that when they were swimming that they brushed against each other and, that Damian had accidentally touched Danny. Something easily done when people are swimming in different directions.

It was that which had prompted Danny to follow Damian because at the children's' home, it was taken as a signal for more of the abuse that he had suffered.

"I'm sorry about that," Damian said. "I hadn't meant anything by it in fact, I can't remember doing it. I've got a lot on my mind at the moment. I'm waiting to hear about a job."

"Oh." Danny put his hand on Damien's leg. "You're really a very nice guy. So kind and I don't have any friends."

"Aren't the people at the home your friends? There must be someone there who you're friendly with."

"No not really." Danny moved his hand nearer to Damian's crotch. "Will you be my friend?"

"Yes, if you want me to." What on earth was going through his mind. Befriending a fourteen year old boy? What would people think? "I'll get us another coffee." This was just an excuse to think. True, he didn't have many friends himself, and on the face of it, there would be no harm done. When he returned to the lounge, he couldn't miss the fact that Danny had now undone the top of his jeans leaving nothing now to the imagination.

"You've got a very kind face."

"Me?" Damian didn't normally rebuff flattery but was quite surprised to hear some from a fourteen year old. "You're not bad yourself." What a statement to make, especially when he had allowed his eyes to rest firmly on the gaping opening in Danny's jeans and the erection that was now quite visible.

Seeing that Damian's eyes were firmly fixed on him, Danny stood up allowing his jeans to fall to his ankles. Not wanting to disappoint him, Damian began to give head to the situation and when Danny turned around, there was nothing else to do but to insert himself into the young boy. After ten minutes the deed was done and both lads got dressed.

"Will you do it to me again if I come round?"

"Next time, you can do it to me," he said as he showed Danny out of the building. "I've got to go out now, so I'll see you soon."

"Will you be swimming tomorrow?"

"I don't know about that. Not if I get this job."

"Where is it?" Damian knew that he shouldn't say anything but the words just came flooding out of his mouth. Danny kissed Damian on the lips and then left.

Deep down Damian knew that this sort of liaison was out of the question. He couldn't go around screwing a fourteen year old boy, even if he was nearly fifteen. What would happen if he suddenly became of age? He could be imprisoned for what they were doing.

All sorts of thoughts and questions were going through his mind as he walked back to Axis. As he walked in, Andrew was just preparing two cafetieres for customers so Damian sat down at one of the tables.

"Hi," Andrew said as he sat down next to Damian. "When can you start?"

"You mean I've got the job?"

"Yes."

"I'll start tomorrow."

Eight

Damian's first morning at the coffee bar could be said to be fairly uneventful. True he had only witnessed the operation on an occasional basis up until then but almost instantly was proving to be an asset, even if a little keen at first. Andrew explained to him that even at very busy times when all of the covers were taken, it was usually better to wait for people to leave before removing the crockery and wiping the tables.

He had arrived early that first morning about ten-thirty. He knew that the coffee bar opened at ten and he had been asked to come in from eleven. The first hour was usually fairly dead, so he would not be needed. It did give him the opportunity to find out where everything was and also to learn how to operate the coffee machine. Something that he might have to do when one of them was on holiday, or when the coffee bar got very busy.

His first task was to make coffee for Andrew, Sam and himself. He had not met Sam before mainly because he worked full time out of town and was only there on his days off. With the coffee car open seven days a week, the three partners worked on a rota basis. Damian would have Tuesdays off and if things were quiet, would finish about six o'clock in the evening. He didn't mind working through the weekend or for six days a week. After all, he needed the money. Sam began to ask Damian why he had chosen to come to Blackpool and the story was again recounted.

"We've been together for ten years," Sam said. "Me and Andrew. It was the best thing that we ever done, moving here."

"It beats London," Andrew said from the

kitchen. "At least up here you can be free."

"True."

"What made you open the coffee bar?"

"Well," Sam added; "it was something that we'd always wanted to do. In time, we'd like a small hotel or guest house. That's our goal and perhaps this might he an avenue into that. We'll have to wait and see how things map out."

"You never know what's around the corner."

"No. I was very unsure about leaving home but knew that I must do it."

"Ah. Customers." Sam had seen a couple of people descending the steps on their way in. They took a table near to the window and Sam served them with their drinks. Just before they left, more people came in and all three of them were busy, until about four o'clock when there was a lull in the constant comings and goings. Time for another coffee break before the tea-time rush.

It was almost half past six before Damian could put on his coat and make his way home. He was by now, feeling quite tired. The coffee bar had never been that busy when he had been there and even the quieter moments were busier than he had previously witnessed.

As he walked up the stone steps, he could see Danny waiting for him on the opposite corner of the road. Damian pretended not to notice him and began to walk home. The last thing that he wanted now was a neurotic schoolboy. He hoped that by ignoring him Danny would go away but, as Damian looked out of his kitchen window on his return home, there was the boy on the other side of the road.

No, he wouldn't invite him in. Why should he? What they had had was a one off in his book. He admitted to himself that he did enjoy it but no way did he want it to

be a regular thing.

It began to rain and like a fool, Damian again looked out of the window. Danny was still there. He began to feel guilty so against his better judgement, went downstairs and opened the door. Danny ran across the road and into the building. Once inside, Damian made coffee and they sat in the lounge. He was not going to let Danny know that he had seen him waiting for him to come out of work and when Danny asked the question, Damian just passed it off by saying that he hadn't seen him.

"I'll get you a towel," he said noticing the rain dripping from Danny's long blond hair onto the carpet. As he walked into the bedroom to get a towel he added; "and you'd better get out of those wet things and put them on the radiators. I'll put the heating on."

"Thanks." Danny undressed and sat on the settee in just a pair of boxer shorts which were quite tight and left nothing to the imagination. When Damian saw him he was determined that nothing was going to happen between them. If it did then, he could find that Danny would be waiting for him every night and that, he definitely didn't want. As they talked each innuendo that Danny made was rebuffed by Damian who was now sitting in an armchair - keeping his distance from the young boy.

"Don't they have a curfew at your home?"

"Yeah. Now that I'm nearly fifteen I'm allowed out until nine but if I'm late, I can always get in provided that I'm prepared to drop 'em for whoever lets me in."

"Oh, I see. They let you in if you're late providing that you bend over."

"Something like that. I don't get screwed every time. Sometimes I just give 'em a blow job. It just depends."

"Haven't you reported this to the warden?"

"No. It's not the sort of thing that you can talk to them about. They know that it goes on and all the older lads say is that it happened to them when they were my age so, now it's my turn. It's just one of those things really."

"What about the other staff or your social worker. Can't they help?"

"You don't understand do you." Danny began to cry. Obviously Damian had hit a raw nerve and quickly tried to change the subject but, it didn't work. Danny wiped his face. "They're at it as well. It's not always one of the older boys that lets me in."

Damian was lost for words. He looked up at the ceiling as if waiting for inspiration but, none was forthcoming. Yes, he recognised the fact that Danny needed help, and that it was help that he couldn't give. He just felt so sorry for Danny. At the same time, secretly wishing that he had been in such an institution. It sounded like fun!

Danny went to the toilet and on his return, he noticed that his shoulders and upper back were quite red. He hadn't noticed this the previous day. The top of his arms looked as if they had been bruised at some time too.

"How did you get those?"

"Oh. Off the carpet." Yes, that would explain the reddening of his back but not the bruising. It was then that he realised that Danny had been roughly treated and had obviously been held down against his will, and raped. Damian's secret wishes suddenly evaporated. That sort of treatment was not right in his book, despite the fact that he had endured similar treatment at the hands of his own brother. He had heard some of the customers in the coffee bar talking about being tied up but almost without exception, they were men in their thirties or older; not a

fourteen year old - even if he did look older than his tender years.

But, what should he do about it? Not get involved. That's the best policy. Then he looked over at Danny. How would he feel if it had happened to him? It had. That afternoon in his brothers' bedroom. That was rape. He did nothing about that probably because he enjoyed it. It was clear that whilst Danny may have enjoyed the sex, the cruelty that went with it must stop. He kept saying to himself, 'don't get involved. It's nothing to do with you'.

Danny looked so helpless, sitting there in just his boxer shorts. He obviously felt safe in Damian's presence, after all, it was Danny that had started things the previous day. Love. That's what was missing from his young friends life. The 'L' word. Perhaps Danny had parents. Perhaps he was at the children's home for reasons other than those that Damian had presumed. Another avenue to pursue, once Danny had calmed down.

Damian disappeared into the kitchen and shortly came back with two glasses. "Here. Drink this."

"What is it?"

"Never mind about that, just drink it."

Danny drank about half the liquid. "This is nice. What is it?"

"Southern Comfort and lemonade. It'll calm you down a bit."

The two boys carried on talking and Damian checked to see how dry Danny's clothes were. He turned them over as they were still quite wet. It would be at least another hour before Danny's clothes were dry. More drinks were poured and Danny had cheered up a bit so, Damian thought that he would ask him about the home.

"How long have you been at that home?"

"Only two years. I was at another one near Preston before that. I got transferred."

"Did that sort of thing go on at the Preston home?"

"I don't know. Well, I think so. It goes on in most homes but I was too young then. No hair," he said pulling the front of his boxer shorts down so that Damian could see all of his pubic hair.

"Oh."

"Once they catch you wanking then, that's when you're given the treatment."

"And that's what happened to you?"

"Yeah. I was in the bog and one of the boys who I thought was my friend looked over the top of the cubicle and saw me. He waited outside for me and that was that. It only took an hour before everyone knew. They caught a lad last week, so I don't get so much of it now, only when I'm late in."

"Why are you there?"

"My parents were killed in a car crash four years ago and my grandmother couldn't have me, so I went into care."

"I'm sorry," Damian said; "I never thought."

"Oh, it doesn't matter. I was never really close to them. Always different. I don't know why. I think that they over protected me, or tried to. It didn't work though."

Damian began to hear metaphoric bells. Yes, he too had felt this way when he was at home, without the over protection although, in a way he could have been. Perhaps that was why his parents were always on at him. Their way of keeping him on the straight and narrow. He now began to feel very guilty about choosing to ignore Danny when he saw him outside Axis, but knew that if he

said anything, it would probably be taken the wrong way and as things have turned out, he knew that he was being of some help - however small.

"Could we watch a video?"

"Yes, if you like. Which one?" Danny walked across to the bookshelves where the video's were and looked along the titles.

"What's this one?"

"I don't know. They came with the flat and I haven't had chance to play them yet. I'll put it on." The tape cassette was in a plain white cover and there was only a number '4' on the cassette label. He put it into the video recorder and switched the television on. The film was about two lads hiking, or at least that was the impression gained by watching the first two or three minutes. It soon became clear that the tape contained a gay pornographic film, and had it not been for both Danny's insistence that they watched it and his own curiosity, Damian would have switched it off.

After ten minutes of watching the film, Danny got up and closed the lounge curtains. As he did so, his erection was plain. Damian's attempts to hide his own failed and remembering what he had said to Danny the previous day, resisted the temptation no more.

Danny finally got dressed and left leaving Damian both confused and worried. It was as if their friendship was beginning to blossom and the company of his young friend was enjoyable. What he was worried about more than anything else was the sex. That would have to stop irrespective of Danny's wishes or desires. He needed however, to do something to stop the wanton abuse that Danny was suffering. How on earth could he do that?

Damian slept very little that night. He just didn't know what to do. The overriding thought was that

he had to do something, but what? The next morning he woke just after nine, showered and dressed. Problem time. Perhaps he had dreamt the solution he didn't know. It could even have been a spark of inspiration. A letter. He would write a letter to Social Services - anonymously of course - and deliver it on his way into work. He had already told Danny that he wouldn't be about for the next two days, in the hope that perhaps Danny would take the hint and latch onto somebody else.

It seemed to work because when he left the coffee bar the following day, there was no sign of Danny and he was not hanging around his flat either. He thought that this was good and then partly regretted sending the letter. He didn't realise that it was his letter that had prompted the home to ground Danny for a week, and that it was this reason only why Damian had been reprieved from the young lads company.

Once the grounding had been lifted, sure enough, there was Danny waiting for him outside work. This time it was not possible for Damian to ignore Danny as he crossed the road and stood in front of him.

"I had to see you," he said. "There're sending me away."

"Where to?"

"To another home near Lancaster. Can we go back to your flat?"

"Sure."

Damian was not worried about this visit because he knew that it would be the last time. Coffee served, Danny told Damian all about the meeting that he had been to with his social worker the previous day.

"They said that someone had told them about the abuse and that they were moving four of us tomorrow to different homes. I don't want to go. I'll miss you."

Fearing another outburst of tears, Damian stepped in to prevent it.

"Just think, although you won't see me, there'll be other kids there that you'll make friends with very quickly. It'll be like a new adventure."

"But I don't want a new adventure."

"Look. When are you fifteen?"

"Next month."

"Well, in just over a year you'll be sixteen. My age. Then you can leave the home and go wherever you want and do whatever you want to. It's not that long to wait."

"But I don't want to go."

"You can write, and I can always come and visit you. Lancaster's not that far away, only an hour or so by train."

"I suppose so. You'll come?"

"Yes. On my days off."

"And if I write, you'll write back?"

"Of course I will. Don't worry." Danny reached over and kissed Damian.

"You're my only friend. You know that."

"I know."

"Can we watch the rest of that video?"

"Ok." Danny turned the tape on.

Clothes were almost ripped off as the two boys again enjoyed each other's body. It was more passionate than before as if they were cementing their relationship. That's certainly what Danny thought as he left Damian's flat for the last time.

It was only two days later that the first letter from Danny arrived. The letter gave Damian a complete run down on the new home, how he hated it and that the regime would be a lot tougher than he had been used to.

The new home was attached to a special school and that he felt cheated in some way. It spoke of their three passionate encounters and that how Danny was missing his new found friend. It was signed, 'Love, Danny.'

Damian left the letter on the dining table and left for work and thought nothing about it until he got home. There on the floor was another letter and over the next three days, eight more arrived, all from Danny. Damian couldn't be doing with all of this. When he had agreed to write to Danny, he had never imagined either the volume or content of the letters that he would receive. Pen had to be put to paper.

Damian had never wrote a 'love' letter in his life before and although he realised that Danny's infatuation with him would wain over the next few weeks as he got settled into his new home, he felt that he would have to let him down gradually. He chose his words carefully, making sure that at no time did he say that he 'loved' Danny, or that there was any commitment on his part towards the young boy. He suspected also that the letters were opened and read before he inmates got them, so he pre-emptied his letter by saying that.

The weather, work and so forth became the content of the letter. No mention was made of their liaison. It was kept to the basics and was as if he was just writing to a friend, not a lover. He did sign the letter, 'Love, Damian' because he felt that he must. On the next one he thought, it would be 'best wishes' only. That way, perhaps Danny would get the message. It didn't work. The letters just kept coming then after about another week of several letters being delivered each day, there was nothing. Three days passed and no letter from Danny. Perhaps in the end the message had finally got across.

That night Damian decided to have an early

night. He had been up until ten o'clock most nights that week and having had a very busy day at work, decided at eight o'clock to have a bath and go to bed early. As he got out of the bath and began to dry himself, the doorbell rang. He had two bells, one - more of a buzzer - for the front door downstairs, and a chime for the one on his flat door. As it wasn't the buzzer, he thought that it was Tony from the flat next door, so having fixed a towel around himself, went and opened the door.

"Danny!" Damian could hardly believe his eyes. There stood Danny and another boy as large as life. "What are you doing here? Come on in." Shocked and annoyed, he let the two boys into the lounge.

"Aren't you pleased to see me?"

"I never expected to------."

"I'll make the coffee. This is Tim."

Damian went back into the bathroom and quickly dried himself. He donned a bath robe and came back into the lounge. He was not amused by having visitors at this time of night, and especially not Danny. Who Tim was, he would yet have to discover! It was when he saw two holdall's on the hall carpet that he began to put two and two together.

"We've run away. I know that you'd be pleased to see me."

"Pleased? Shocked, yes. Who's Tim? Is he from the home as well?"

"Yeah. He was moved with me to Lancaster. We've both come back. Neither of us can take it anymore. I knew you'd understand."

"No. I don't understand."

"But you ran away."

"That was from home and I was sixteen. You can't just run away from a children's home and not expect

anyone to come looking for you. If the staff have seen my letters to you, they'll have my address. This is the first place that they'll look. You stupid idiot! Didn't you realise that? You're not that stupid are you?"

"No. We're not stupid. They've not seen the letter so they haven't got your address. Don't worry."

"Bloody hell!"

"You're not pleased to see us are you."

"It's not a case of being pleased or otherwise. Yes, it's nice to see you, but it's just that it's a shock. That's all. I mean, where are you going to stay? You've got to sleep somewhere. You've got to eat."

"We can stay here, can't we?"

"It's a one bedroomed flat. I've only got a double bed. I can't put you up even if I wanted to."

"You don't want to?"

"It's not that I don't want to." Damian just didn't know what to say or do about the situation. If he called the police or social services, then his liaison with Danny would come out, and that was something that he must keep quiet. "What about Tim? They'll be worried about him, won't they?"

"No," Tim replied. "I'm sixteen next week anyway."

"That's not the point. You just can't run away."

The boys drank their coffee in silence. Damian just didn't know what to do. He knew that he would have to put the boys up for the night and that he would have to sort them out in the morning. There was nothing else that he could do. Faced with this inevitability, he suggested that the boys bathed as he hadn't yet pulled the plug out on his bath water which was still quite hot.

Tim went first and while he was bathing, Damian took Danny into the kitchen and after closing the

door, gave him a bollocking for being what was in his mind, totally stupid. He added that he would put them up for the night and that they would be sent back in the morning.

"We'll wait for the morning. And Danny, I mean it."

Danny began to realise that he had been very stupid and that he shouldn't have just left the home. Boy, would he be in for a bollocking when he got back. He wanted to see Damian and his tunnel vision and actions had now dropped both himself and Tim right in it. Tim came out of the bathroom wearing just a towel and then it was Danny's turn to ablute.

"I'm sorry if we've put you out," Tim said, sitting down on the settee.

"I've just spoken to Danny. We'll sort it out in the morning. Where we're all going to sleep I don't know."

"Together?" Tim suggested.

"It'll be too cramped."

"Not if we all cuddle up together." Damian nearly choked on his coffee. "Or, you could always make Danny sleep on here." A glazed expression crossed Damian's face. Had he heard right? Was Tim actually suggesting that the two of them slept together? Ignoring the comment but not the growing erection that Tim was eager to display, Damian said that perhaps they might all get into the bed, the settee not being very comfortable to sleep on.

When Danny came out of the bathroom, he suggested that they should watch a video and yes, he chose the same one as before. Nothing happened while they were watching it other than arousal but it stood them in good stead for the night ahead!

Nine

Damian awoke about eight o'clock the next morning. Danny was still sound asleep, but there was no sign of Tim. Quickly getting into his bath robe, he went through into the kitchen. Tim was already there and the kettle had just boiled. He made both of them coffee but couldn't resist giving Damian some pleasure before they went into the lounge. He knew that it was time to really lay the law down to the two runaways, so when Danny finally appeared some thirty minutes later, the ultimatum was given.

"You've got to go back to the home and, I mean today." The two boys looked quite pathetic in their expressions, both realising that Damian meant what he said. "So, we'll all get dressed and on my way to work, I'll make sure that you get on the train. No excuses."

"Didn't you want us to come and visit?"

"Danny, you just can't run away from the home. Yes, it was nice to see you, both of you but; you've got to go back. There's no alternative."

"What if we don't?"

"If you don't go back then, I'll have to tell social services. They will come and get you and take you back. Perhaps even to a secure unit and, none of us want that."

"But you said you'd come and visit me."

"I know and I will, but I only have one day off each week. I will come and visit you providing, you promise me that you won't do anything as stupid as this again. Danny?"

"I promise."

"Tim?"

"And me."

"Right. Get dressed and then we'll go."

The boys did as Damian instructed and within half an hour were on the train back to Lancaster. Just in case they decided to divert, he notified the Station Master that there were two boys on the train and that they had run away from the Springfield's Children's Home in Lancaster and asked if he could pass on the message. The Station Master seemed quite concerned but complied with Damian's request. The last thing that Damian wanted was for the boys to be back at his flat that night or for that matter, any night. Before he had to do any explaining, he left the railway station and headed onto work at the Axis coffee bar.

When he arrived Dave let him in and then he proceeded to get on with his work. Dave and Andrew asked him if he was all right as he seemed to them to be preoccupied. He didn't want to lie, so he told them about the nights events. The only thing he didn't mention were the ages of the two runaways. They both felt that he had made the right decision in allowing them to spend the one night and returning them as soon as it was practicable to do so.

Another busy day ensued followed by four more before he had his day off. This one would be spent in and around Blackpool and following a stroll on the Promenade, he thought that he would walk along Central Walk, just to see if there was any action. By now he had met quite a lot of people, but with the exception of Tony, none of them could really be called friends. To his surprise, there was no action at all so rather than just hang about on the off chance, he went back to his flat.

The infatuation that Danny had shown in Damian began to wain over the next few weeks. The

letters went from being daily to weekly, and the contents
became much of a general rather than a sexual nature.
Damian was quite pleased about that because he had
always felt that even though Danny may be gay, he was
too young to get into any kind of relationship. He too felt
that he was happy living on his own only pleasing himself
and, no longer dependent upon anyone else for his own
personal survival.

True, Keith his landlord quite often required his
services and Damian felt that he needed time to grow up
before making any sort of commitment to another person.
He enjoyed having his own space, something that he had
never had the luxury of, until now. Work kept him off the
streets and he was gradually re-building his life.

Towards the end of August, a Thursday. Work
as usual. He didn't know that it would be that day that
would change his life, forever. About four o'clock, he
managed to sit down with Dave and Sam for a quiet
coffee. Nearest to the servery when a customer came in,
he served them and then went back to the 'staff' table. A
young lad of about nineteen had come in ordered a
cafetiere of coffee and seemed to be looking at the video
playing on the four television screens. Every time Damian
looked in the guy's direction, it was as if he was staring at
Damian. Eventually the guy paid and left. 'Strange
bloke', he thought but put him to the back of his mind
until he was almost ready to leave for the day, when the
lad came back in.

Curiosity roused, Damian got himself a coffee
and sat down at the next table to the young lad so that they
had their backs to each other. Sensing something, Sam
struck up a conversation with the customer. This was
usual practice anyway, but having seen Damian shyly sit
down at the neighbouring table, enquired perhaps deeper

than he would normally have done. The young man was very attractive and like Damian, had quite a baby face, looking much younger than his years.

"Are you here on holiday?" Sam asked.

"Yes. Two weeks."

"Have you come far?"

"Lincoln. Well, just outside. Didn't fancy Skegness this year."

"To be honest, I don't fancy Skegness any year. I'm sure that it's a nice place but, it's not for me. Are you staying local?"

"I've booking into the bed and breakfast place over the road for a couple of days. Just while I find somewhere better. It's my first time in Blackpool, so I didn't really know where to go to get information."

"Well, there's a variety of hotels that cater for gay clientele and some of them are exclusive. Have a think about it and take a card away if you like."

"Thank you I will. Are you staying local?" he said turning round to face Damian.

"No. I live in Blackpool and work here. I'm just on my way home."

"Hard day?"

"We've been very busy. Nonstop from eleven to four. Going home to relax now."

"Not after a hard night then."

"I'm never that lucky. Mind you, I don't usually go out on the scene, so what should I expect." Damian got up to leave, only to be followed by the young lad.

"Do you mind if I walk with you?"

"No. Not at all. I'm not very good company though. Not after being on my feet all day."

"You could probably do with a massage."

"Probably. I'll get round to it one day."

"I do massage."

"Do you? How much?"

"I usually charge twenty pounds for a basic massage."

"I couldn't afford that."

"But I'm on holiday. I never charge when I'm on holiday or away from work."

Damian just couldn't stop himself from inviting Paul back to his flat. He was still very naive about such matters and didn't realise that in the gay sense, a massage usually involves sex, or leads that way.

"Your shoulders are very stiff," Paul said feeling Damian's shoulders as he opened his flat door. "I can certainly do something with those."

"Oh good. I've never had a massage before. What should I do?"

"Well, you need to be laying down, so either on the carpet or the bed. Whichever you prefer."

"Don't you have to be on a hard surface? Every time I've seen them on telly, they always seem to be. Not that I'm bothered."

"It's better if you are on a hard surface. Just put a towel on the carpet and we can do it in here." Damian laid out a towel on the carpet and laid down on it. "You need to take your shirt off though. I can't massage you through that with much success."

"Sorry. I never thought of that." Damian removed his shirt and laid down again. "Is that any better," he asked .

"Yes. Lay on your front, head to one side and I'll start. Tell me if I hurt. Sometimes it's difficult to assess."

"OK."

Paul began to massage Damian's shoulders, pressing gently on the tender young flesh. He started moving to his spine and all down his neck and back. It felt good and Damian could feel the tension of the last few weeks gradually leaving. Paul rubbed in some massage oil into Damian's skin and then turned him over so that he was laying on his back. His rib cage was next and then to his legs. Paul tried to push Damian's jeans out of the way of his legs but they kept falling down. In the end Damian undid his jeans and raised himself so that they could be pulled off. Once legs had been done, Damian was turned again so that the buttocks could be worked on under his boxer shorts. He began to groan as each cheek was carefully rubbed and separated from the other.

"Now it's your turn," Paul said carefully taking his silk shirt off.

"But I've never done it before."

"It's easy. Just do what I did and you'll be fine." Damian did as he had been asked and yes, it was easy at first but his hands soon got tired. He worked his hands all over Paul's torso and legs. He wasn't too sure of the buttocks but gave it a go anyway. When he had finished, Paul turned over onto his back and looked up at Damian. "Lay here," he said. Damian did so. "You missed a bit."

"Where?" Damian thought that he'd covered all of Paul's body.

"I've still got my briefs on. You missed that bit." Paul took them off and laid back on the towel.

Damian began to caress Paul's eager tool, all eight inches of it. First by hand and then by mouth. He worked away until satisfaction was imminent at which point, Paul whispered, "wait;" and then brought Damian to the same point. They looked at each other, their eyes

sparkling. This had been something else. Damian had never experienced such tenderness coupled with such strong sexual pleasure.

"Now what shall we do?" Paul asked, not wishing to impose himself upon his new found friend.

"Anything you like," Damian replied. Paul stood up and placed his knees either side of Damian's torso. As he knelt there Damian got ready to suck him into oblivion. Instead, Paul lowered himself so that be became impaled on Damian until he exploded into him. Almost at the same time and without further manipulation, Paul shot all over Damian. Exhausted, the two boys held each other tightly and kissed. Neither wanting to release the other from their grasp.

"How was that?"

"Fantastic." Damian didn't know what else to say. All he could do was to lay there next to Paul kissing and caressing him. He just didn't want to let him go. Where had he been all of his life. Realising that Paul would probably now want to go, Damian suggested coffee. Paul followed him into the kitchen and with his elbows on the work-top, stared into Damian's eyes. The look was returned and Damian kissed him again.

"You're beautiful," he said. Damian knew that he was attractive but not beautiful.

As the two boys made their way back into the lounge, Damian noticed that Paul appeared to be crying. He couldn't understand why and it was only when they had cuddled up together on the settee that Paul gently started to drop the bombshell.

"I know that we've only just met but, do you have a boyfriend at the moment?"

"Me? No. Not a regular one. I've seen a young lad on a couple of occasions but, no one regular."

"Oh. Would I be able to see you again?"

"Of course. You were fantastic. I don't think that I've ever had it that good."

"I'm not that good at it. It's just that, well, it's not every day you meet someone that is as nice and kind as you are."

"Kind? I don't understand." Damian was very confused by Paul's comments. He didn't know him at all. How can you be kind where all you've done is to have sex with a guy. Gentle perhaps but, kind?

"Yes, kind. Let's face it, most people you meet just want a quick hand or blow job and head for the nearest bog or quiet place. You don't know me but you've allowed me into your home and yes, made me feel very special."

"There must be guys back home in Lincoln who would make you feel special too. I can't be the only one."

"If I'm honest, no. That was the best that I've ever had. Yeah, I've had many guys over the years, but that was special. Very special. You are special."

Damian smiled. A cat who had just got the cream would not have had a bigger smile. He had enjoyed himself too. A fact that he couldn't hide, nor wanted to. Perhaps it was partly due to the fact that from the first moment that he saw Paul in Axis, there had been a stirring in his loins and some form of attraction. Otherwise, why would he have sat down at the next table and not gone straight home.

He wanted Paul. Having set out to get him, he had baited the line well and finally hauled him in. What a catch. The surprising thing was that Damian hadn't really realised what he was doing other than the fact that he knew that this must not be just a one night stand. He had fancied Paul rotten. Had he flirted with him? He had seen

that go on all the time in Axis. 'Single' guys sitting along at tables waiting for Mr. Right to come along and then leaving at the same time as another single guy.

Paul was hooked, he knew that. His feelings too seemed to put him on cloud nine. Yes, it had been the best sex that he had ever had and he fancied Paul. He also knew just how predatory the scene in Blackpool was, and might have to make a presumptuous move if he wanted to keep him. Did he want to keep him? What would the point in that be because he then remembered that Paul was only here for two weeks and, that if they got too serious, then he would be devastated when Paul had to go back home.

"I don't want to go," Paul whispered into Damian's ear.

"I don't want you to, but I know that you must." Damian began to cry. Could this actually be love? He didn't know. All he knew was that he didn't want to get off the settee and get dressed. He felt safe in Paul's arms.

"Yes," Paul sighed. "I suppose that I must."

"Why don't you stay the night?"

"I'd love to, really I would but perhaps I should go back to the hotel. I could always see you tomorrow. That way it will give us both time to think."

Damian resigned himself to the fact and the two boys eventually got dressed, not before another romp on the carpet. Sadly, Damian opened the flat door to let Paul out. They stood on the doorstep and gazed into each others eyes. This was more than just a casual pickup. Both of them thought that. Paul gave Damian a long goodnight kiss.

"I love you," he said as he turned and walked down the stairs. Damian burst into tears as he saw Paul leave the building. He went back into the flat and sat

down on the settee and fell asleep.

The next morning, Damian woke later than usual. It was almost ten o'clock. He showered and then spent almost half an hour deciding what he would wear. He tried on four different pairs of jeans before deciding which pair to wear and almost every top that he had. Today would be special and he wanted to look his best. By the time he arrived at the Axis coffee bar, Paul was already there, sitting at a table in the back section. Damian ran up to him like a wild animal striking at its prey. He embraced Paul and kissed him. 'Yes', he thought to himself; 'today would be special'.

Paul stayed all day and every time that Damian managed a break, instead of sitting on the 'staff' table, he went and sat with Paul. Their conversation became very intense as the day wore on, and sensing that there was 'love in the air', Andrew suggested that Damian should finish at five o'clock that night as they were quiet. They went down to the Promenade and Paul bought hamburgers which they ate sitting on a bench near the war memorial.

"Did you mean what you said last night?" Damian enquired. "That you loved me." Paul got up and walked around for a minute. He then faced Damian and again stared straight into his eyes.

"Yes. I did." He carried on walking about. "I couldn't get to sleep last night thinking about you. You're the best thing that ever happened to me."

"You are to me." Damian remembered through the vale of love that Paul would be going back home. "How often do you come to Blackpool?"

"This is my first time. It's a beautiful place. I wish that I'd come before."

"How far is Lincoln?"

"I don't know. About a hundred miles or so.

Why?"

"Well, I was just thinking about when you go back."

"But I'm not going back."

"You're not?"

"No. There's no way that I can go back home. Not now. Not unless you come with me." He sat back down on the bench. "That's why I didn't get much sleep last night. I couldn't think about anything but you and I've never felt like this about anyone."

"Wow!" Damian could hardly believe his ears. Paul was actually prepared to leave home because of him? Could he be that special? "But Paul----."

"No. I've made my mind up. The only way for me to be happy is with you. Nobody else, you. Can't you see that? I really do love you."

Paul lit cigarettes for both of them and they sat in silence for what seemed an age but in reality was only a minute or so.

"Well," Damian said standing up. "If you're going to move in, we'd better get your stuff from the hotel." Paul looked stunned for a moment before his expression changed to happiness. Both had grins that a Cheshire cat would have been proud of. Damian offered his hand to Paul and ignoring anyone that may have been about, walked off arm in arm to collect Paul's clothes.

"Do you mean it?" Paul asked.

"Yes. I love you too."

Ten

Damian and Paul's relationship blossomed. The two lads were inseparable. They had no secrets from each other except one. Damian had told Paul that he was just eighteen. He knew that if he had told Paul of his true age, then there would have been no relationship at all. They may not even have got together on that first date.

The winter months had contributed to their loving lifestyle. Bad weather is one of the main reasons why people stay in, read a book or watch television - or have sex. It was as if they just couldn't get enough of each other, proceeding to hop in and out of bed at all hours of the day and night. Paul had managed to get a job working behind the bar at Bodgers and even though it was only for a couple of nights a week, they managed to financially survive.

Fate had obviously dealt them a good hand during the festive season which for them, seemed to be and endless round of parties either for Halloween, Christmas or New Year. Valentine's Day came and went as did Easter. Easter had never meant much for either of the two lads before but in 1996, it did. It heralded the start of the early summer season in Blackpool giving rise to an almost doubling of the population and an increase of customers at the Axis coffee bar. They seemed to be on the go from their ten o'clock opening until closing time somewhere between seven and eight in the evening.

Paul didn't spend so much time in the coffee bar but when he wasn't working, always met Damian. When the met, each had a aura which spilled over onto the other one. Love was not only present, but there for the whole world to see. They would hold hands walking

down the street and exchange kisses on many occasions. There were no worries. A match made in heaven. The sort of relationship that both gay and straight couples strive for.

In the April, Paul seemed to show signs of tiredness, not with Damian but within himself. He had developed a dry cough which seemed to come and go and began to skip meals. Damian thought nothing about this until one Thursday, Paul was not there to meet him from work. He knew this was odd and hung around outside the coffee bar for almost half an hour. There was no sign of Paul. Damian decided to walk home. As he opened the downstairs door, Tony was waiting for him.

"Damian. Thank God you're here."

"What's wrong? Paul!" Damian tried to run past Tony but he held him fast. "Paul!" Tony slapped Damian across the face. He didn't really want to do this but it was the only way that he could get Damian to listen to him.

"It's all right. Paul's in bed, asleep. Come into my flat."

"No. I must see him."

"He's sleeping and needs to. Come on." Reluctantly, Damian went into Tony's flat. "Sit down and drink this," Tony said handing a large Southern Comfort to Damian.

"What's wrong?"

"You'll stay there?"

"Yes. What's wrong? Why can't I see Paul?"

"He's not well. He was coming out to meet you from work, and well he just collapsed in the doorway. I've put him to bed and given him a couple of aspirin to help him sleep. He was sweating a lot. It's probably just a bug."

"He's been sweating a lot the last couple of nights."

"Temperature?"

"Up, I think. Is he OK though?"

"He'll be fine but he needs his sleep. Your trouser snake won't be shooting any venom tonight."

"It hasn't for a couple of nights. Paul's been so tired. He does work hard and he's overdone it a bit, that's all."

"Yeah. That's all it is. Don't worry, in a couple of days, he'll be fine."

"Perhaps I should call the doctor."

"I don't think so. Leave it for a day or so then, if there's no improvement, call him then. You don't want to get him out on a wild goose chase, do you."

"No." Damian thought for a minute. "I want to see him. Will you come with me?"

"Yes."

Tony and Damian went next door to see how Paul was. As Tony had said, Paul was sleeping. He was very hot and had discarded the duvet. The bedclothes were wet through with sweat. Although he looked quite angelic sleeping like a baby, Tony started to get a little concerned.

"Let's go back to mine."

When they had got back into Tony's flat, it was Tony who suggested that they should perhaps call out the doctor. Tony gave Damian another drink while they were waiting for the doctor to arrive. Because neither of the lads had registered with a doctor, Tony called his own doctor and because it was after hours, the locum emergency doctor came out within the hour, just. Damian was beginning to panic as the doctor examined his lover. Paul was barely conscious as Damian held his hand.

"How long have you been together?" the doctor asked.

"Just over ten months."

"Mmm. And how long has he been like this?"

"He's been off colour for a week or so but, he would be with a viral infection; wouldn't he?" The doctor looked up at Damian and could see the tears flowing down his cheeks.

"Yes. That's right. It's just a viral infection but because of his high temperature, I think that we'd better send him off to hospital for a check up."

"No! You can't take him away from me!"

"Damian," Tony said; "nobody is taking him away from you. He's just going into hospital so that he will get better."

"I must go with him." The doctor looked again at Damian.

"You can go with him. I need to telephone for an ambulance. Perhaps you could pack a bag of things that he'll need."

"Yes. Of course."

Tony held a bag open while Damian quickly got things out of drawers. Razor and toothpaste from the bathroom, a change of underwear and socks, and a clean shirt and trousers for afterwards. The doctor had used Tony's 'phone and in less than ten minutes, the ambulance arrived. While the crew were getting Paul ready, the doctor had a quiet word with Tony, who then announced that he would come as well.

"Thank you. The doctors given me a couple of pills to calm me down a bit."

"I'll lock up and meet you downstairs."

When they arrived at the hospital, Damian registered Paul's arrival. The receptionist didn't even bat

an eyelid when he explained that they were an affair. She did say that the doctor would need to speak to him later but for now, all he could think about was Paul. All sort of thoughts were going through his young head. Could it have been something that he had eaten. No, they had shared meals so, if it was that then, he too would surely have been struck down. He remembered that Paul had been waiting in the rain the other night for him and that they both got soaked through on the way home. No. He ruled that out too.

It seemed hours before the doctor came out of the room where Paul had been taken. In reality, it had only been three-quarters of an hour. He looked at the two lads sitting on the bench, eagerly waiting for news. They were taken into a side room and sat down.

"How is he?" Damian asked.

"Well, Paul is quite ill but we've managed to stabilise his condition for the moment. We'll be keeping him in for a couple of days at least until his temperature comes down to an acceptable level."

"But it can't be that serious! Why haven't I got it?"

"I can't say. It's probably just a viral infection that's really got hold of him and if we keep him in then, we'll be able to make sure that he stabilises correctly."

"Why can't he come home?"

"We need to give him some very powerful antibiotics and they come in drip form not tablets. I'm afraid that it's not just a question of my prescribing a bottle of tablets so that he could take two, four times a day. We do really need to keep a careful eye on him. You can stay here if you want to and I'll let you know when we're transferring him to a ward." The doctor left.

"He'll be all right Damian, you'll see."

"But I want him at home. I can't stay here all the time, can I."

"No but, while you're at work, I can come and visit him so that he won't be on his own."

"Would you?"

"Yes, of course I will. We all love him you know."

"I know. Thanks Tony."

Some twenty minutes later a nurse came into the room to say that Paul was being transferred to the ward. Tony gathered up the bag that they had brought with them and they followed Paul as he was wheeled through the hospital. Once the nursing staff had settled him into bed, the lads were allowed to sit at the side of the bed.

Three bottles of fluid were hanging up on the drip stand and the tubes led all the way down to a canula which had been inserted into the back of his left hand. Paul could barely open his eyes because he had been given a hefty sedative whilst in the admissions department. All Damian could do was to hold Paul's hand. How peaceful he looked. Laying there fast asleep, totally oblivious to all that was going on around him.

Damian and Tony were allowed to stay until nine o'clock, at which time they had to leave. Tony suggested that they walked home, thinking that it would allow Damian to get some much needed fresh air. He had been devastated by Paul's hospitalisation. When they arrived back at their flats, Tony helped Damian to change the sweat sodden sheets on the bed and insisted that they both got an early night. Damian gave Tony a spare key to his flat so that he could come in the following morning. As it turned out, Damian was already up and dressed at eight o'clock when Tony did come in.

"Morning."

"Hi Tony. Kettle's just boiled. Can I use your 'phone?"

"Yes. I 'phoned an hour ago but all they would tell me was that he had a comfortable night."

Damian went next door to 'phone the hospital. Tony had just made himself a coffee when he returned.

"How is he?"

"They want me to go down to the hospital."

"What for? Is he ready to come home?"

"No. They think that they know what it is that's made him ill, but they wouldn't tell me over the phone and want me to go down."

"Oh, yes. It's just the confidentiality thing."

"Yeah but, they want me to have some tests too."

"In case you may come down with it."

"Something like that. They said to come down after lunch."

"But you're working."

"I'll get time off. That shouldn't be too much of a problem. I'll go in and see Andrew. I'm sure that he'll understand."

Damian went into the coffee bar and worked until two o'clock. He had been given as much time off as he needed but agreed to come back after going to the hospital. Tony said that he would go with Damian to the hospital and came into the coffee bar just before two. Andrew had given Damian a ten pound note to cover the cost of taxi fares saying that he could 'pay it back at some time'.

Somewhat nervously, the lads entered the ward and spoke to the nurse in charge. It wasn't the same one as the night before, so there was a certain amount of

explanation that was required. Having been told that Paul was beginning to respond to treatment, she said that the doctor wanted to see Damian and that they should wait in the waiting room while she bleeped him. She would not allow them to see Paul until the doctor had spoken to them.

Damian began to get very worried despite the fact that the nurse had made it clear to him that Paul had begun to respond to treatment.   It was about fifteen minutes later when the doctor arrived.

"Do you mind if we speak in front of your friend?" he asked as he closed the door.

"I'll wait outside if you like."

"I think that it might be better if you did." Damian's eyes visibly widened. What on earth was the doctor going to say that couldn't be said in front of Tony. "Now then Damian. How long has Paul been ill?"

"Only a couple of days. Why?"

"Could you tell me what relationship you are to Paul?"

"I'm his boyfriend, and he's mine." There was no hesitation in his voice. Why should there be. He was proud of their relationship and was not going to deny it, even to the doctor who may, be one of those who didn't approve of such things.

"I see. And, what sort of sexual activity took place between you?"

"What do you mean?"

"Was your relationship of a sexual nature."

"Oh yes."

"And," the doctor was obviously having trouble with his own embarrassment in asking the questions. Knowing it to be a very sensitive area and in his eyes, unconventional. "Would that activity include both oral

and anal?"

"Yes. Why? What's that got to do with him catching the flu?"

"Please bear with me. Was there give and take on both sides?"

"Yes. I don't understand. What are you getting at?" A nurse opened the door and brought in a tray of cups. She left and then returned with a coffee pot. Instead of leaving, she poured three cups of coffee and then sat down next to Damian. "He won't tell me what's going on."

"Last night after you left," she began; "we ran some tests on Paul."

"What sort of tests?"

"Blood tests. We found out that he has a viral infection."

"That's why he's on all of those drip things."

"That's right," the doctor said; "but, we have been able to identify the virus. It is the Human Immunodeficiency Virus."

"That sounds serious."

"I'm afraid that it is. Do you know what it is?"

"No. What was it again?"

"Human Immunodeficiency Virus."

"That's a mouthful."

"It is, that's why we shorten it when we talk about it. To HIV."

"HIV?"

"Yes. Do you know what it is?"

"No. Not really. I've heard it talked about but I've got no idea what it is."

"Do you mind if your friend comes in now, I think that he may help you."

"No. He can come in. We don't have any

secrets from each other. HIV?"

As Tony came back into the room, Damian suddenly clasped his hands to his face. His memory had just jerked into place. Surely it couldn't be *that* HIV. He was convinced that it wasn't but slowly became glazed as the penny finally began to drop."

"Tony. Paul's OK. He's only got HIV." Tony went over to Damian and held him so tight that he could only just breath.

"I'm sorry Damian. I'm so sorry," he said trying to comfort Damian and not to allow the traces of tears to be seen.

"It's not *that* HIV is it Tony?"

"Yes. I'm afraid that it is."

"We'll come back." the doctor said and both he and the nurse left the room. Damian broke down and the noise of them both crying could be heard down the corridor. About ten minutes later the doctor came back into the room.

"I'm sorry to disturb you," he said as the lads looked up in the direction of the door; "but, we need to get you tested. Just as a precaution."

"When?" Tony asked.

"Now if possible. Will you both need a test?"

"No," Damian said confidently.

"It's been six months since my last one. That was negative."

"We'll test you both."

While Tony had been out of the room he had been talking to the nurse on duty at the desk and had told her that he had in the past, had a sexual relationship with Damian although only brief. She had told Tony of the diagnosis before he had come back into the consulting room

The nurse took both the both down to pathology where their blood samples were taken. She explained that under normal circumstances it would take twenty-four hours for the results to come back, but because it related to Paul's admission, then the results would be back on a few hours. Tony suggested that they should come back later but Damian wanted to see Paul.

"They won't let you see him until the results of your blood test."

"Why not?"

"Well, look. There's no easy way to say this. If you've got it, then there is no need for you to take precautions. If you haven't got it, then you will need to take precautions."

"I only want to see him. I'm not going to jump into bed with him!"

"I know. I don't mean condoms you idiot! Sorry. I didn't mean that. Look. When we go back for the results, have a word with one of the counsellor people. They'll explain it to you a lot better than I can."

Damian didn't know what to do. Despite his tender years, he had grown up very quickly following his move but the shock of realising that his lover was so ill, restored him to no more than a quivering wreck. He couldn't think straight and was very distraught. The whole of his world seemed as if it was falling apart around him and that there was nothing that he could do to prevent it happening.

Tony decided to take him into Bodgers. It would be a way of passing the four hours that they had to wait and at times like these, he had always advocated a drop of the hard stuff to ease the pain. Damian wasn't really in the mood for a drink but needed something to take him out of himself. If anything happened to Paul, he

had no idea what he would do. He didn't even know how Paul could have caught the virus.

Their sex life had been such that he would have known if Paul had been unable to perform so was sure in his own mind that he hadn't been with anyone else. Neither had Damian. Since Paul had moved in, he too had kept the relationship monogamous. He only hoped that perhaps the hospital had got it wrong and that when his test result came up negative, that they would retest Paul and find that his too would be negative.

The hours slowly passed by and as the two boys returned to the hospital Damian confessed to Tony that he was very frightened.

"Don't worry. You'll be in the clear. I'll go in first."

After ten minutes in the consulting room, Tony came out.

"Well?" Damian enquired.

"I'm OK. Now it's your turn."

Some thirty minutes later Damian came out from seeing the doctor.

"See," Tony said. "I told you that it would be OK."

Damian shook his head, went very pale as the news that he too had HIV began to sink in, and he collapsed in a heap in the floor.

Eleven

During the next five weeks, Damian visited Paul every day in hospital. Every time that the subject of HIV was mentioned by Paul, Damian would seek to change the subject because he had decided that he wouldn't tell Paul that he too had the virus, until his loved one was back at home. Those weeks had been pure hell. Tony had been great, popping in every day at least twice to see how Damian was coping. Apart from a loss of appetite, Damian showed no other signs of being ill. From the outside, nobody would have known of his plight.

As with all cases of positive diagnosis, the hospital in addition to informing the patients doctor, also recommend that the patient makes contact with a local Body Positive group or similar voluntary organisation. This is so that they can get help and advice as well as sharing their experiences with others. Damian had made contact although, he did have to be taken along to the group by Tony, who was already a volunteer member. When he was down, he could telephone them and talk over his problems any time of the day or night.

On one occasion, he telephoned about three o'clock in the morning and just cried. The people there were a great avenue of support, and gave him advice on where to go from here, and reassured him that having the virus is one thing. Getting an Aids diagnosis was altogether something else, and that he should not dwell on that possibility at all. It would be years away, not imminent so, basically, carry on with life and don't worry.

Paul too had received both counselling and visits from members of the group although Damian didn't know this and had been told on his first visit to the group that he could well meet people in their centre who could

well choose to ignore him in the street. This he found difficult to comprehend until it was explained that it was for confidentiality reasons and that some of the volunteers chose to operate in that way.

It was on one of his routine visits during the sixth week of Paul's stay in hospital that Damian was asked to speak with the doctor. He had chatted to the nurses and bought them a few boxes of chocolates for all of their time and trouble looking after Paul, but this was the first time that the doctor had asked to see him. He sat patiently waiting in the ward reception area waiting to be called in. Yes. Today was the day that Paul would be coming home. That's why the doctor wanted to see him. About twenty minutes later, the doctor arrived on the ward and asked Damian to go with him into his ward office.

"Please sit down Damian."

"Is he coming home today?" Forever the optimist.

"That's what I need to talk to you about." Damian began to get excited. "Have you said anything to Paul about your own condition?"

"Not yet. I thought it better to wait until I'd got him back home. He's bound to get upset, and it's not really nice for that to happen here."

"I see. Well," the doctor thought for a moment. "I think that the time's right for you to tell him now. He's bound to suspect."

"Why? Has something already been said?"

"No. Let me explain. Paul's had the virus for some time. It wasn't something that he picked up in Blackpool. He's been HIV positive for about three years. That much we know."

"How?"

"Well, we do ask about people's sexual partners

in a case like this, and two of the people who were on Paul's list have both died from the disease. They progressed to having an Aids diagnosis and in one case, had that diagnosis before they met Paul."

"What does that prove?"

"It means that the infection that Paul's got it a little more serious than we first thought. Let me explain. In this country, you start off with the HIV diagnosis. You have the virus in your immune system and it will either stay dormant for ever, stay dormant for a few years, or will act immediately and cause other problems. When we talk about an Aids diagnosis, we mean that the patient has HIV and also two other related diseases or illnesses. In Paul's case, he has developed Pneumocystis Carinii Pneumonia or PCP for short. This is a chest infection and is quite common amongst people with HIV."

"Yes but you can treat that with anti-biotics can't you."

"We can certainly prescribe drugs for that but, there is no direct cure. In addition to PCP, we believe that we have found traces of Cytomegalovirus, CMV."

"So what are you saying? Paul's developed a chest infection?"

"No. It's like a mathematical equation. HIV plus PCP plus CMV mean that we have to change our diagnosis."

"You mean he's OK."

"No, I mean that we now have to give him a diagnosis of Aids."

Damian stared into space. He had discovered through his contact with Body Positive that HIV and Aids were two different things although, one could lead to another in some cases. The doctor looked at Damian who by now was visibly shaking. He left him alone for a few

minutes after which, the traditional therapeutic tea had been obtained by one of the ward nurses. He knew deep down what this meant. Although approaching seventeen, he had grown up very quickly since leaving home, and was now neither innocent or stupid; two terms that could have described his initial naivety.

"Damian. Do you understand?" The doctor had to ask despite being able to see the tears running down his face. "I'm very sorry."

"Sorry!"

"Yes I am. We all are."

"But you've just told me that he's going to die."

"Not necessarily." Damian looked up. "It is true that we know that Aids is a killer but many people survive years after being diagnosed."

"But he's still going to die, isn't he."

"I'm afraid so."

"Does he know?"

"Not yet, although we can't hold off telling him for much longer. I wanted to talk to you first as you'll probably want to be there when we do."

"Yes. He'll need me. More than ever now."

The doctor left Damian to take in the bad news. It had been his worst fear. All of the people that he had met since receiving his own HIV positive diagnosis had said, perhaps deliberately as an afterthought that HIV can lead to Aids, but never in his wildest dreams did he think that Paul would progress to that stage.

He also knew that he would have to think about himself as well. So far, everything that he had done was with the view that Paul would come out of hospital, would be well and that their life together would be long and happy.

After twenty minutes a nurse came in and asked

Damian if he wanted to see Paul. He said that he did and the nurse took him to the private room where Paul had been moved. They kissed and hugged each other for what seemed ages when the doctor came in.

"How are we today Paul? Feeling a little groggy?"

"Yes."

"Well, we'll try and make you as comfortable as we can."

"Have you got it?" Paul asked Damian who's face dropped giving the game away.

"Yeah. They tested me the day you came in. Don't worry though. I'm looking after myself and you'll be home soon anyway." Tears began to fall down both their faces.

"Now Paul. I have something to tell you," the doctor began.

"It's the big one isn't it."

"We've diagnosed PCP and we think that CMV is also present. I'm sorry that there's no easy way to tell you this."

"It's Aids. I know. I heard you talking about it to one of the nurses last night. You left the door open. Has Damian got it?"

"I'm HIV positive. That's all. For now."

"I'm so sorry. I must have given it to you."

"That's not important. You're going to get better. That's what's going to happen. Don't you lay there worrying about me. I'll be all right."

The doctor left and the two lads held each other tight. Paul felt guilty that he had given the virus to Damian. That if his diagnosis had gone from just being positive to Aids then, how long would it be before Damian too was going to be told that his death sentence had been

confirmed. Tony would have to be told. He couldn't keep that sort of thing away from him. He'd been too good to both of them for that.

Damian stayed at the hospital until eight o'clock that night. All he wanted to do now was to go home and to cry. He had been quite good at keeping his emotions away from Paul as he didn't want him to see just how devastated he was. As he went through the flat door, he began to look around. There were all the things that they had bought together. Their photographs on the top of the television. The ornaments over the fireplace. Then there were all of Paul's clothes. Everywhere he looked, there was the evidence of Paul. The guy that he had chosen to spend the rest of his life with.

Would he ever come home? Damian fell on the bed and began to cry. His whole world seemed to be falling all around him. It was as if he had been ripped apart. Other then the inevitable, what on earth could go wrong next.

The next nine weeks were spent visiting Paul. He spent as much time with him as he could. It didn't take a doctor to notice that Paul's condition was gradually getting worse. Sometimes the changes were slight and sometimes more obvious. One day the drip stand would only have one bottle on it, then two. His visits were not interrupted every hour now but, every twenty minutes by a nurse checking Paul's temperature and pulse. His colour began to change and his vision began to deteriorate. Damian knew that he would have to prepare himself to be able to cope with Paul's imminent death. All he would have to do would be to wait for a telephone call either at the coffee bar or to Tony's flat.

The lads who ran the Axis coffee bar were very good to Damian allowing him as much time off as he

needed. Every time that the telephone rang, his heart would miss a beat. It did however give him something to occupy his mind. He felt that he ought to tell the lads about his own status and thought that he would immediately lose his job, but didn't.

Although they were shocked by his own diagnosis, they already knew of several people who had also been unlucky enough to contract the virus and to them, it made no difference. Yes, Damian had been a little treasure to them. An asset that they did not want to lose. The conversations that he had with the customers also took his mind off things and by now, was beginning to stop worrying every time the telephone bell went off.

Christmas was looming. His second Christmas away from home and he feared, away from Paul. The coffee bar would close for both Christmas Day and Boxing Day, so he would be able to spend all day with his deteriorating lover. He had already spoken to the hospital to see if Paul could come home for Christmas and whilst they said that it would be a good idea, were apprehensive. Yes, they felt that it could be very therapeutic for Paul to spend a couple of days at home but were worried in case Damian couldn't cope with the endless care that Paul would need. In the end, they said that they would assess his situation a couple of days before and if stable, would allow a stay of thirty-six hours beginning in the evening of Christmas Eve.

Damian was already preparing by buying decorations, a large tree and a few goodies that they could eat. He would spoil Paul because deep down, he knew that it would be their first and only Christmas together. That fact would not spoil it for either of them. He would put it to the back of his mind until after the festivities had ended.

Tuesday 17th December was his last day off before Christmas. He spent the morning shopping and the afternoon with Paul. By now Paul was completely blind. Damian had made a point of always wearing his favourite aftershave every time now that he went to see Paul so that he would know when he was there. He left as usual about eight o'clock and made his way back to the flat. As he turned the key in the outside door, he could see Tony waiting on the landing.

"Hi," he said as he raced up the stairs. "He's a bit better today."

"Good," said Tony unconvincingly. "Come and have a coffee." Damian had reported almost every day to Tony to tell him about Paul's 'progress' but felt that on this occasion Tony wasn't his normal bubbly self. He sat Damian down and held him firmly by the hand. "I've just had a 'phone call from the hospital," he said as he began to cry. "Just after you left, Paul died."

"No, he's fine."

"Damian listen to me! He's at peace now. No more pain. I'm so sorry. They want you to go back. To see him. To say goodbye."

"He's not--------."

"Yes he is Damian."

Damian let out the loudest possibly yell and burst into tears. Tony held him close as the shock finally began to sink in. For over an hour they remained in each others arms, consoling each other. Several Southern Comforts later, Tony finally persuaded Damian that he must go to the hospital and that he would go with him.

"I'd like to see him as well. He was a good friend."

"Yes. Yes you must. He would have wanted that."

"I'll 'phone for a taxi."

When the two lads arrived at the hospital, they first of all made their way up to the ward where Paul had been. They were told that he had been moved to the mortuary and given directions on how to get there. Damian was too distraught to take Paul's belongings with him so Tony said that they would pick them up on the way back from the mortuary. The staff seemed to be quite surprised by Paul's sudden downturn as despite being ill, tried in his own way to cheer up the other patients. Even that stopped once he was moved to a private room.

As they entered the mortuary, the attendant folded down the shroud that up until then had been covering Paul's face.

"He's at peace now, Damian. At peace."

"I know," Damian replied desperately trying to hold back the tears. "At peace."

"You can touch him or kiss him if you want to."

"Yes."

Tony leant over Paul's body and kissed the forehead. He could feel himself about to cry, so he left the room. This would also give Damian a few minutes alone with Paul. He needed to say goodbye. Perhaps to bring it home to him that Paul had finally gone or, to allow him a few moments of private grief. Before leaving he kissed Paul both on the forehead and on the lips, by which time he was so distraught that he had to be helped from the room by the mortuary attendant.

"Come on Damian," Tony said as they left the mortuary and made their way back to the ward. "We've got to get Paul's things." He held Damian close to him as they went back to the ward. The doctor stopped them in the corridor and offered his condolences. Seeing the state that Damian was in, gave him some tablets to make him

sleep. He gave them to Tony. One of the nurses handed Damian a parcel that contained Paul's clothes and possessions. He didn't really want to know, so Tony took the parcel.

Having taken a taxi home, Tony made sure that Damian was all right before he left him. He stood over Damian while he took the tablets that the doctor had given him, all the time asking, "why? Why Paul?" Tony didn't have an answer and was very reluctant in leaving Damian alone.

"Shall I stop with you tonight?"

"No thanks. You've done enough. I'll have some hot milk and go to bed. See you in the morning."

"You get into bed first and I'll get your milk." Tony realised that if he hadn't insisted on this, Damian would have spent the night pacing about the flat and not getting any sleep at all. That would not do because the next day would be quite traumatic for Damian as arrangements would have to be made. Paul's family would have to be contacted.

Tony was quite tired but waited until Damian dropped off to sleep before leaving him alone. He went back to his flat and decided that for him too, sleep might just be the best medicine.

Twelve

Thanks mainly due to the alcohol that had been consumed during the previous day, and the sleeping tablets handed out by the doctor, Damian managed to get quite a good night's sleep. He emerged with quite a hangover though and slipping his robe around himself, made his way to the kitchen. He had only just managed to fill the kettle and to set it to boil when Tony let himself in. The two lads looked at each other and then Tony flung his arms around Damian. This was the catalyst that prompted both the lads to cry. Innocent tears for an innocent life, taken so early as to be unbelievable.

"Is it true?" Damian asked.

"Yes. It wasn't a dream. Come on. Paul wouldn't have wanted all this fuss and besides that, we've got things to do." Tony knew that whilst he must show compassion, he also had to be quite firm with Damian otherwise, they would get nowhere.

"Such as?"

"Look. You go and get yourself dressed and I'll make the coffee."

Damian went back into the bedroom. Tony knew that his neighbour would not have the strength to cope on his own, so had managed to clear most of his own arrangements for that day in order to be with Damian. The last thing that he wanted to do was to leave Damian alone, if it could be helped. He was unsure himself of exactly what would need to be done but knew that the first priority was for Damian to make contact with Tony's family, to tell them the sad news. With a bit of luck, they may decide to undertake all the necessary arrangements. This would take most of the pressure off Damian, and that

could only be good.

Eventually Damian made an appearance and the two of them took their mugs of coffee into Tony's flat so that the telephone call could be made.

"Would you rather I did it?" Tony enquired.

"No. It's really down to me. Thanks all the same. I do appreciate it. I'm not looking forward to it though."

"No. I don't suppose you are."

Damian finally plucked up enough courage to make the call. Again the tears began to flood down his boyish cheeks. As he lifted the receiver, oh; how he wished that he would dial a wrong number or, that Paul's parents would be out. Whilst Paul had spoken of them quite a lot, Damian had never spoken to them, even though he knew that they were aware of him.

The call was made and Paul's father said that he would drive to Blackpool that day and would meet up with Damian that evening. Tony's telephone number was left as a contact point and still wiping the tears from his eyes, sat down on Tony's settee, head in hands. Tony telephoned the Axis coffee bar to say that Damian wouldn't be in because of Paul's death and then made Damian another coffee.

While Damian had been left alone with Paul the previous evening, Tony had enquired at the hospital of what arrangements would have to be made. He was told that a post mortem would be needed before the body could be released to a funeral director but, that the death certificate needed to be obtained from the hospital before the death could be registered. That was something that either Damian or Paul's father would have to undertake.

As he looked at Damian sitting so dejected and alone on the settee, he knew that something would have to

be done in order to take him out of the spiral of depression that he knew only too well, Damian had begun to withdraw into.

Knowing that things and indeed life had to go on despite this very personal tragedy, he suggested that a trip to the hospital to collect the death certificate and to register the death might prove to be a useful way of getting Damian to sort himself out.

"Look love," he said. "You can sit there all day if you want to but, don't you think that we should be doing something?"

"I know. I'm sorry. I just don't know what else to do."

"Yeah. I can understand that, but there are arrangements that need to be made."

"Oh, for the funeral."

"Well, yes but, other things as well."

Tony explained about the conversation that he had had at the hospital the night before and Damian insisted that it should be he who registered the death. After a few minutes, the two lads set off for the hospital and then on to the registrar. Rather than get a taxi which would have shortened their journey time considerably, they opted to walk. The fresh air bouncing on Damian's young cheeks had the effect of waking him up to the fact that life indeed must go on, despite the fact that deep down, he did wonder just how long it would be before he too, would be no more.

Once they had registered the death, Tony suggested that they went for coffee. Axis was the nearest so, off they went. As they walked down the stone steps down to the black doorway, Andrew noticed Damian and rushed to the door to offer his condolences. More tears began to ooze.

They sat up the corner of the coffee bar as customer after customer came up to Damian to say just how sorry they were. By now the tears had stopped and Damian seemed to begin to accept the fact that Paul was no more and, that he would have to again pick himself up, dust himself off and indeed, start all over again.

In his mind, he knew that he could never forget Paul. The love that they had both shared was something that would take time to get over. After all, he couldn't now just go out and meet other people because of his own status. Neither could he go out cottaging to pay the rent.

At the back of his mind there was the malicious thought that perhaps as someone had given HIV to Paul, that he should avenge his death by having unprotected sex with anyone and everyone in order to pass the virus on. He knew that he just couldn't be that irresponsible, despite the thought that in some way, it just might avenge having his lover taken away from him. What was he to do.

That evening was by chance the monthly meeting of Body Positive and despite already having tendered his apologies in order that he could spend more time with Paul, he decided to go along to the meeting. He knew that he would also have to meet Paul's father later on, so he arranged with Tony to make the arrangements for the meeting when the phone call was received.

"Are you sure that you don't mind?"

"Of course I don't. You go to the meeting and I'll come and get you when Paul's father rings me and, I'll come with you to meet him. I'm not letting you do that on your own."

"Thanks. I won't forget this you know."

"Look. You would do the same for me, wouldn't you?"

"Yes."

"Well then. Don't worry about it."

"But your clients?"

"They can wait. If I get that desperate, there's always the five fingered shuffle." Damian smiled for the first time since receiving the news. "That's better. I know that your very upset, devastated even, but life does have to go on."

"I know. You're right of course. Just me being silly."

"Not silly. Just you, being you."

"Yeah. My turn to get the coffee."

After an hour or so in the coffee bar, the lads decided to return to their flats. It was almost tea time and neither of them had eaten so far that day. Having made sure that Damian would be all right, Tony left him and went into his own flat. He would need to be there to receive the phone call from Paul's father so, was quite anxious to return home and not to miss him.

Damian got himself a sandwich and then showered and dressed ready for the meeting. Very apprehensively, he set out on the fifteen minutes walk to their meeting room. Once there, he told the co-ordinator about Paul's death who had already heard about it from the hospital. Charles had been down to the hospital to visit two friends that day and had intended to call in to see Paul afterwards. Damian was quite happy because on this occasion, there were no tears, just hugs from those present.

Although it was an ordinary monthly meeting, Charles opened the meeting by suggesting that they had a minute or two of silence to remember Paul and to pray for Damian. Once concluded, the meeting took its course until just before nine o'clock when Tony peeped round the door. Apologising for disturbing the events, Damian knew that it was time for him to leave, so after receiving yet

another round of hugs from those present, left the building.

"Where are we meeting him?" Damian enquired as they walked quickly towards Winter Gardens.

"Outside St. Johns' church," Tony replied checking his watch to make sure that they weren't going to be late. "I didn't know anywhere else to suggest that he might know. Mind you, if he's never been to Blackpool before, then he might have difficulty finding that."

"Did you say that it was opposite the Winter Gardens?"

"Yes. He said that he had seen the church as he drove through to his hotel. I didn't catch everything that he said although, I got the impression that he came in on the wrong road because he's staying somewhere in South Shore."

As they approached the Winter Gardens, they saw a man standing outside the church. He looked from that distance to be about thirty years old and had a very short haircut.

"What are we going to do?" Damian asked. "If we just go up to him, someone may well think that we're after trade. Anyway, it can't be him, he's too young."

"It must be him. There's nobody else there on their own. Come with me and I'll start talking to him."

"Ok."

As they got nearer to the man, they realised that it must be Paul's father; despite the haircut and looking much younger than his forty-two years.

"Hi. I'm Tony and this is Damian. Are you David Fellows?"

"Yes. It's very nice to meet you both," he said offering his hand to each of the lads in turn. "I only wish that we could have met under better circumstances."

David gave Damian a special hug.

"Do you mind if we go to a pub? There's one just around the corner."

"No. That's fine."

The three of them set off for Bodgers which was only a matter of a couple of minutes walk away from where they had met. Small talk was the order of the day, discussing the weather, David's journey and, what he thought of Blackpool. Paul was not mentioned. Although Damian thought that this was strange, for a father not to mention his son, but once they had got inside Bodgers and had sat down with three pints of lager, it did start to become clear.

David felt very embarrassed about meeting the two lads. Talking to them in a gay pub only served to compound the embarrassment, but he knew only too well that he couldn't put off talking about Paul any longer.

"I hope they don't think that I've picked you two up," he said in an attempt to break the ice.

"Oh no," Tony replied. "Most of the people know us both and knew Paul very well. You might get one or two funny looks but don't worry about it. It's strange at first, after all, I presume that this is the first gay pub that you've ever been into."

"Not quite the first, but I don't make a habit of it. Paul took me into one in Lincoln. It was where he told me that he was gay. He thought that I'd make a scene, and he wanted to be on territory where he felt safe. I don't know why he didn't tell his mother and me at home. We both knew, or at least suspected that he was gay so, it didn't really come as any surprise."

"Oh I see."

"Anyway. Like it or not, we need to talk business. There are arrangements that need to be made

and, well, having talked the matter over with his mother, we feel that it would be wrong of us just to have the body taken back to Lincoln. We may not have approved of Paul being gay or of his relationship with young Damian, but if we know our son as well as we think we did, it's quite probable that he would have wanted Damian to have some say in the arrangements. We don't want to take it totally out of his hands, but do need to have some input into it."

"I see." Tony couldn't understand why David Fellows seemed to be talking to him, and ignoring Damian. Not that he minded because he didn't feel that Damian was up to doing a lot of the talking anyway. He thought that perhaps he would relax with another pint inside him, so he left David and Damian alone while he went to the bar to replenish their glasses.

"I am really sorry you know. Not just for Paul but for you as well. It must have been a shock."

"It was. I'd been to the hospital that night to see him but, it must have happened while I was travelling home. If I'd have known that it could have happened that quick, I wouldn't have left him. We both wanted to be together at the end and even talked about it a couple of times. Strange really. I did love him you know. Really I did. It wasn't just a sexual thing."

"I know. He wrote to us a few weeks ago and told us all about you. It would be just before he went into hospital. I suppose it's a couple of months now."

"Oh I see."

"Well, we had to write to him to tell him that one of his friends had died of the same thing. He may have told you."

"No. He didn't mention it and I never read his private letters. Not unless he showed them to me."

"I see."

Tony returned with the drinks.

"Now down to business. The wife and I have always said that we wished to be cremated." Damian tried to interrupt. "Just hang on a minute young man. We know that Paul didn't, s, that only leaves us with burial. We have to respect his wishes. It costs about the same, so it's of no matter to us. The question is, should we take him back home and do it all from there, or should we arrange for someone local to do it."

"But I assumed that he would go back to Lincoln."

"Not necessarily Damian. Although it will cost us to come up here for the funeral, we're quite happy to do that if you feel that would be what Paul would have wanted." David paused to take a large gulp of his lager. "It's a bloody good pint, I'll say that. Anyway, because we've seen nothing of Paul in the last few months and more importantly, if he hadn't have caught that blasted virus off some dirty so and so, he would have settled here and outlived us all, probably. That's why we feel that it should be your decision, Damian."

"Up here, please." Damian was very surprised by David's offer.

"Well, if you did love him as much as you say you did, then that's settled. Do you feel up to making all of the arrangements? I know it's come as one hell of a shock. It has to his mother and I although, we suspected after his friend died of it that it wouldn't be all that long before Paul got it. I suppose that he's passed it onto you."

"Yes, but I don't mind."

"Well, his mother and I will pay all of the funeral costs so, you won't have to worry about any of that, but we're not rich, an, they'll be nothing left over for shall we say, compensation."

"I don't want your money Mr. Fellows. I want Paul. He's all that mattered to me now and if I can't have him at home anymore, I want him somewhere so that I can still go and talk to him whenever I want to."

"I didn't mean to upset you. I'm sorry. That all came out wrong. I didn't mean to offend."

"I don't think you did Mr. Fellows it's just that, Damian's not really over the initial shock yet."

"No. I should have realised. Look Tony," he said fumbling in his pocket for a piece of paper to write down his address and telephone number on; "here's the address and I think you've already got the phone number. It's better if I go now and leave you to make all the arrangements. I'm staying at the Autumn Grange Hotel. If you can let me know tomorrow early, which undertaker you're going to use then, I'll call round there on my way back home just to confirm everything."

"Yes. Of course. Have a pleasant trip."

David emptied his glass, shook both their hands and then left.

"I'm glad that's over," Damian said, as David made a swift exit.

"Yeah. Too right! Pompous git."

"I know. Bloody insulting at one point although, I suppose that it couldn't have been easy for him."

"True. Anyway. We'd better be going as well. You could do with an early night and tomorrow is going to be a very busy day."

"You're right. I've about had it."

"I'll get us a cab."

Tony went off to arrange for a taxi to pick them up and deposit them at their flats. It was quite a traumatic experience meeting Paul's father. He knew that it had

affected him and he wasn't the one closest to Paul. Goodness knows how Damian must have felt.

The next morning, Tony telephoned a local undertaker and then spoke to David to advise him which firm would be dealing with the funeral. Tony had said that both he and Damian would visit later that afternoon to finalise everything, which they did. The church was booked, the vicar engaged, the graveyard notified, the date agreed. In order to save time, they called into the vicarage on the way back to discuss the service. That then gave them four days in which to relax to await the day of the funeral.

The day before the funeral, Paul's family arrived. Damian, who by this time had got over his initial shock and trauma, met them off the train. Tony had planned to go with him but due to unforeseen circumstances, wasn't able to do so. All went well and after what he considered to be a surprising round of hugs and kisses, Damian saw them all off into taxis. They had not been able to all stay at the same hotel but had booked into three different hotels, all as luck would have it, in the same street. David asked to meet Damian later that day at the flat, just to go over the final arrangements.

Eventually, time ticked itself by and Damian woke the next morning quite early. Indeed, he had already drunk five large mugs of black tea before Tony came knocking on the door just after ten o'clock.

"Hi," he said letting himself in with the spare key that he had been given. "Is everything ready?"

"I think so. I don't know just how many people are coming. The family will be here about half past, or so David said last night. He brought those bottles so we could all have a drink before we leave."

"Blimey!" Tony exclaimed as he turned to see

about thirty bottles lined up on the wall unit. "I hope that we don't get through that lot."

"No. It was very good of him. I must admit that I hadn't even thought of drinks beforehand."

"Well, at least they'll be plenty to go round."

"Will you come with me in the first car?"

"I'm not family. It's direct family that travels in the first car."

"As good as. You were like a brother to him and, I would really appreciate it."

"Well, we'll see what David says."

"It's got nothing to do with him, really."

Tony realised that things were starting to get on top of Damian. Over the last three days or so he had come out of his protective shell quite well, but it was clear that things were now coming to a head. He sat Damian down with a large Southern Comfort, in the hope that it would calm him down. It seemed to do the trick because moments later, earlier than expected, Paul's family arrived.

The conversation revolved around small talk. Most were embarrassed by the fact that Paul was gay, and to die of what the unwashed, uneducated general public tended to consider a 'gay disease', seemed to be too much for them to cope with. Damian spent most of the time in the kitchen producing endless cups of tea and coffee, leaving Tony to do the hostess side. Eventually, there was a knock on the door and they all left for the church.

Damian was very surprised when the car pulled up outside the church because there seemed to be dozens of people just milling about. He looked at his watch. Were they too early or was the previous funeral just coming out. Neither, as it turned out were true. He clung to Tony as he waited in line for Paul's coffin to be carried

into the church. As he followed the coffin down the main aisle of the church, he realised that the people who had been waiting outside, were in fact there to pay their respects to Paul, and couldn't get in because the church was full. It seated nearly a hundred.

The service lasted about twenty minutes before it was again time to follow his loved one out of the church. As he looked up, he could see members of the congregation whose lives had been touched in some way by Paul and thought to himself that, perhaps when it was his turn to be carried out of church, that some of them might be there then. He would like that.

Since leaving home that morning, he had not shed one tear. Most of the family had done so and Damian felt that Tony too had succumbed. He hadn't. Feeling that he would completely crack up if he did, found the inner strength from somewhere to hold the tears back. Oh, he wanted to cry, if there were any more that he could shed. He didn't have to wait too long.

The ten minute drive to Layton Cemetery seemed to take ages but once there, the coffin was placed at the side of the grave ready for the vicar to say the final words. Beforehand, the undertakers places a single cross of flowers on top of the coffin. In the newspaper notice of Paul's death, Damian had asked for donations to be sent to the local Body Positive group in lieu of flowers and was quite surprised of the number of wreaths and bouquets that had still been sent. It took the undertakers quite some time to sort out the cross of flowers that Damian had sent.

Once the coffin had been lowered and the service ended, all of the mourners just waited in silence. Damian didn't want to be the first one to move. Even now, he didn't want to leave Paul. It was then that Tony picked up a handful of earth from the pile next to the grave

and gave it to Damian. Then Damian remembered that he had to throw the earth on top of the coffin, as a signal to other family members to do likewise. Waterworks time. He could hold back no longer. Tony held Damian quite firm on fear that he just might fall into the grave because he had edged nearer to the hole to say his final goodbye. As he turned to Tony, he just couldn't help himself and the tears came flooding down his face.

Tony tried to walk Damian away but he refused and wouldn't be moved until everyone else had left the graveside. He knew that he was holding up the proceedings but wanted to spend just that extra few minutes to allow his emotions to flow.

"You can come back whenever you like."

"I know, that's why I wouldn't have him cremated. I'll have to come and talk to him again. I can't leave him here, alone, all by himself."

"But he's not there anymore Damian. His body is yes, but his spirit is now with God."

"Do you really think so?"

"I know so. He'll be watching you from on high. Just think of that. He may not be here in person, but he'll always be with you."

"I hope so."

As the gravediggers approached wishing to fill in the grave, Tony managed to get Damian back to the waiting cars. All that remained now was the wake. Bodgers had been good enough to offer to do a buffet for them, so as perhaps Paul would have wished, that was where they all headed for.

Thirteen

Over the next few months Damian tended to keep himself very much to himself. Another period of withdrawal followed Paul's tragic death. His job was going well and at times during the main summer season, had struggled to get more than one day a week off. Everyone had been so supportive towards him, even afraid to speak in the early days; just in case Damian was likely to explode into tears before them. All that had now past and Damian was beginning again to get used to the idea of living alone.

He found it so difficult to keep up a positive mental attitude, especially when he went on his weekly visits to Paul's grave. By now a headstone and kerb had been placed on the grave, and while he changed the flowers for the ones that he made a special point of buying from a local gay florist, he used to sit quietly on one corner of the kerb, just looking down at the blue chippings that lay on the slab. After a while he would look at the inscription and then back down to the blue chippings.

There was not usually a lot to say to Paul, but he would always make the effort to tell him about what he was doing, if he had seen any of Paul's special friends, or if he had received a letter from Paul's parents. That, he would sit and read to him. Even in death, there would be no secrets between them.

Damian was growing up fast. Now approaching the ripe old age of eighteen, his attitude towards life had developed. This may have been in part due to his HIV status. Quite wisely, he realised that everyone had an HIV status, it was just that he was one of the growing number who had become positive. The world and his cat may be

negative but he was positive.

At times he treated it as if he had been awarded a gong in the New Years honours list. Not proud but, he was one of the few; as he saw it. It was one way of coping with the knowledge that one day, he too would be laying in a cemetery grave. He felt special. He was special. What he and Paul had was special. That, he could never forget but desperately needed someone to love, and to be loved by.

The weeks and months seemed to fly by until Christmas seemed to be just around the corner again. This immediately brought with it the thoughts of the previous year, and another wave of depression. He knew that this would be a difficult time, so in order to ensure that his day off coincided with the anniversary of Paul's death, he went to the florist as usual and bought an extra special bunch of flowers and a small wreath.

There was no conversation this day. With flowers placed, he carefully removed some of the blue chippings from the slab so that he could kiss it. Perhaps a final goodbye. As he replaced the chippings, he placed three in his coat pocket thinking that he would place them in a small dish on the lounge windowsill, so that he could have a constant reminder in the house. After all, the weather just might get so bad that he wouldn't be able to make his weekly trips.

As he looked up from the grave, he noticed several other people tending graves of their loved ones or friends. How quiet it was. All he needed to do now was to get some fresh water for the flowers and would then be on his way. When he returned to Paul's grave, he saw another lad about fifty yards away. Paying little attention, he completed his tasks and decided to leave.

It had now begun to rain, so rather than walk

back into Blackpool, he decided to catch a bus. As he entered the bus shelter, he saw the lad who he had seen earlier. He was very upset.

"Hello," Damian said somewhat tentatively.

"Hi. Not a nice place is it?"

"Not really. I've got a friend that's buried here."

"Both my parents are in there. Dad died three weeks ago. It came as such a shock."

"I'm sorry. I didn't realise."

"It's Ok. I'm getting used to it now. I'd only just got over mum's death when the old man had a heart attack. My fault. I shouldn't have told him."

"You can't blame yourself. It's only nature taking its course."

"I know that really but, I shouldn't."

Damian half wished that he'd never said anything. He thought that he could have only made things worse, or if not, increased the level of upset that the lad was feeling. Even though he didn't really feel up to it, he did wonder if in some way he could cheer the lad up. Perhaps they could go for a cup of coffee or something. He dare not really suggest it and didn't need to because the lad spoke first.

"Are you going into town?"

"Yes."

"Busy?"

"No, not really."

"Fancy a drink?" Damian was quite surprised by the lads offer but felt that as he obviously wanted or needed to talk, he couldn't really refuse.

"Yes," he said hesitantly. "I think I could do with a pint."

"Good." The lad poked his head out from the

bus shelter. "It's stopped raining now. Fancy a walk?"

"Why not. I usually do. I'm Damian by the way and no, I don't have three sixes tattooed on my head."

"Right. I'm Richard." They shook hands. "I know a place just off Church Street. Well, Talbot Road really. It may not be your sort of place but I like it."

"Yeah. Anywhere."

As the two lads turned off Talbot Road into Cookson Street, Damian began to wonder where they were heading. Richard pointed out the building when they were a couple of hundred yards away.

"That's it. On the corner."

"Oh, you mean Bodgers."

"You know it?"

"Yes. I've not been in for some time but, I used to use it quite often."

"Is this where you and your friend used to come?"

"You could say that. Before he went into hospital, we used to be in most nights. Mind you, then I had to drink coke with a straw and dip it in his pint when the staff weren't looking. They serve me now even though I'm not eighteen for another six weeks."

"I never thought of that. It's a good dodge! I'm just nineteen. How old was your friend?"

"He would be twenty now. It was one year ago today that he died."

"Bloody hell! Sorry. You must be in as much need as I am."

"Not that far off."

"I should have asked first but, you don't mind being seen with me, do you?"

"No. Why?"

"Well, you know what people are like. Two

walk in together and they're an item."

"No. It doesn't bother me, if it doesn't you. Here we are."

The two lads went into Bodgers and ordered two pints of lager. Richard told Damian all about his parents and about how they had been very close to each other until, Richard had decided to come out and to tell them that he was gay.

"Why do you think that they reacted like that?" Damian enquired.

"Well, dad used to be a coal miner before we moved to Blackpool, and well, I suppose it was the fact that having a poof for a son cast doubts or reflected on him in some way or another. Mum wasn't so bad about it. She wouldn't tell dad. That was something that I would have to do."

"So why did you move out of home?"

"Well, after I'd plucked up the courage to tell my dad, he started making life difficult for me. You know, every time Lily Savage came on television, he'd say something like; 'It won't be long before you're doing that'. It really hurt and when a friend of mine said that there was a bedsitter going close to where he lived, I thought that I'd take it. What about you? How did your parents react?"

"Pass. I never told them that I was gay. My brother knew, or at least guessed but, I could never have told them. We didn't get on all that well. I just left home on my sixteenth birthday. Couldn't wait to get away from there."

"At sixteen? Blimey. I would never have had the courage to do that, not at that age anyway. I struggled when I did move."

"Yeah. It was a struggle. The worst thing was

that I'd mapped it out in my own mind what I was going to do, but even when I was at the railway station waiting for the train, I began to have second thoughts."

"But you wouldn't know what lay ahead. Why Blackpool?"

"I don't know really. I stood in the queue at the ticket office and I hadn't a clue where to go. I knew that I wasn't going to go to London, and just happen to see a poster advertising Blackpool Tower, so I thought yes. Why not. That's why I'm here."

The conversation continued for another hour or so before Damian said that he had to get back to the flat. He explained that he only had the one day off each week and that if he didn't get his washing done, then he'd have nothing to wear for work in the morning. Damian thanked Richard for the drink, shook him by the hand, and left. The real reason why he needed to leave was because he had got a hospital appointment later that afternoon and didn't want to say anything to Richard, just in case he ran off.

During the walk to the hospital, he began to think that he quite liked Richard and that he hoped that he would meet him again sometime. Yes, perhaps in time, he could become a close friend. He would like that, and despite what Richard had said, Damian felt that he had most definitely been 'picked up'. A broad smile crept across his face and he felt a warm glow inside of him. He thought how nice it was to feel that other people were still attracted to him. Then, he thought of Paul. The memories came flooding back.

Knowing that deep down he still had a lot of affection for Paul, he had begun to realise that life must go on and Paul at least, would not expect him to be celibate for the rest of his life. What on earth would he do if he

was to meet Richard again and, more importantly, what would he do if Richard made a pass at him. Would he succumb? How could he? He had a positive status. Surely that would be the end of his sex life other than the frequent five fingered shuffles that he had enjoyed so much over the last year or so. There must be a way around it, he thought as he approached the clinic. He would ask the consultant about it.

Damian felt quite chirpy as he came out of the clinic. All his test results showed no deterioration in his condition, and the consultant had put his mind at rest. Now all he would have to do would be to buy some condoms, but how. He had never bought any in his life before and remembered the stories from school of the older boys going into chemist shops for them, and because they were served by a female, coming out with tubes of toothpaste or fruit lozenge's.

The weather had changed and it was now raining quite heavily so, Damian caught a bus into the main bus station. As he came out and began to walk down Talbot Road, he saw a chemist shop on the corner. Peering through the window like a naughty schoolboy, he could see that there were only female staff, and that the condoms were on the counter. Knowing that he already had several tubes of toothpaste in the cupboard at home, he walked straight up to the counter, picked up a three pack, paid his money and then left. He could feel his face glowing bright red as he left the shop. Surely everyone in the street must have known what he had bought. But why should he feel embarrassed? Surely this was a sign of maturity and of responsibility. Never the less, he decided to call into the Axis coffee bar on the way home.

Andrew was very kind to him as always and because it was fairly quiet, sat down with Damian who

proceeded then to tell him all about Richard, and asked for his advice.

"It's not really a problem, Damian. Is it."

"Well yes. I haven't told him that I'm positive."

"But that shouldn't make any difference at all. OK, you've got to take precautions if you have sex together but, if he likes you and you like him, continue the friendship."

"Yeah, but as soon as I tell him, he'll run a mile. He won't want to know."

"Look at it from this point of view. Let's say for a minute that you and Richard get close and decide for whatever reason that it's time to get between the sheets. Then you've got to tell him."

"Then he runs away."

"Not necessarily. He may be surprised, too surprised to be able to carry on then but, if you talk it through, you might find that he stays. If he does do a runner then, at least no harm will be done, other than both your prides being hurt a little. Nothing more. If that happened to me then, I wouldn't want to know him."

"I suppose you're right. In a way."

"Nobody knows how anybody will react to that sort of news. Let's be honest, there are people out there who are that ignorant of the facts that they would run away from that sort of situation but, there are others who will not. They'll say that it doesn't matter and take precautions. Safe sex rules, OK. Once over that first hurdle, you then have another to climb."

"What's that?"

"Well, either he's just after your body and it'll be just a one night stand, or he'll come back for more of the same and then who knows."

"I see. I'd never thought about it like that before. I thought that I'd never be able to get it together again, with anyone."

"Nonsense and you know that it is. You're young, very attractive and, from what Paul said on a couple of occasions, quite a babe in bed."

"True. That's the other problem, Paul."

"Damian. Paul's been dead now for a year. Look at it from the other side of the coin. If you had died and Paul had been left, how would you feel if he decided to live a celibate lifestyle. Would you want him to do that?"

"No."

"Well then. Haven't you just answered your own question?"

"I suppose that I have."

"I'll get us another coffee."

Damian began to think about what Andrew had said. Yes, if the boot had been on the other foot, he wouldn't have wanted Paul to live the rest of his life on his own. A life of celibacy. No, that would be the last thing that he would have wanted. He also wouldn't want to be forgotten. Damian knew that he could never forget Paul then, he remembered that his school friend Jason's mother had remarried after his father had died in a car crash. Love does live on inside all of us. We never forget our first real love but, we all move on to new partners when tragedy falls.

"Here," Andrew said as he put the coffee down on the table. "Sorry I was so long, I had to put some more through."

"That's Ok. It's given me time to think."

"Good. I mean, having said all of that, I wouldn't suggest that you rush into anything. Make sure

that it's what you both really want before taking steps, yeah."

"Yeah."

"Anyway.   When are we going to see this gorgeous hunk?"

"Don't know.   We didn't make any plans to meet up again. I'll probably see him about sometime."

"Get out there and find him. I know that you met in very auspicious circumstances, but if he took you for a drink then, whilst he probably wasn't wanting sex in return, he did like you."

"But he didn't know me from Adam."

"I know but, how many times have you got chatting to someone in a bus queue and then invited them for a drink if you didn't fancy them."

"You're right. It's just that---------."

"It's Paul, isn't it?"

"Yeah."

"Well, I think that we've not put that one to bed. Yes?"

"Yes."

"You'll never forget Paul, never. He won't forget you either. Have you thought that he might be steering you into going out and meeting people. He can still see you and is watching over you, so don't feel guilty about anything."

Andrew gave Damian a hug just before he left for his flat. On the way home he thought of nothing else but of the conversation that he'd had with Andrew, and in the cold light of day, just how much sense it made. He was being silly thinking that his status should prevent him from going out and meeting people.   Friends were desperately needed. A bedfellow would also be nice. He should have arranged to meet Richard again.

The next three weeks went by with no sign of Richard. Damian made his weekly visits to Paul's grave and again no sign of Richard. On his way home this Thursday, he passed by The Hanging Stiletto pub and sitting outside was a familiar person. He wasn't sure if it was Richard, so pretending not to notice him, he slowly walked down the road on the opposite side. There didn't seem to be any response, so after twenty yards or so, he allowed his bunch of keys to fall out of his pocket. As he picked them up, he could hear someone calling his name. He stopped and turned around.

"Hi," he said as Richard approached.

"Damian. I haven't seen you for weeks. How's it going?"

"Not bad, I suppose."

"I must have missed you at the cemetery this morning. I was a bit earlier than usual."

"Oh," Damian exclaimed. "Were you looking for me then?"

"Well, you seemed such a nice guy when we met last. I thought that I'd like to see you again."

"Yes. Fancy a coffee?"

"Yeah. The lager here's like piss water today. Probably near the end of the barrel. Coffee would be nice."

"Good. There's a nice coffee bar that I know, or we could always go back to my place."

"Whichever. Perhaps your place, if you don't mind. At least then if we're talking we won't be overheard."

"Ok."

The two lads set off on the fifteen minute walk to Damian's flat. They laughed and joked most of the way there, almost with the ease that comes from a long

standing friendship.

As Damian opened the flat door, he picked up three items of post that had been delivered and, putting them carefully on the kitchen table, switched on the central heating and then the kettle.

"Grab a seat," Damian said pushing the lounge door open. "The place is a tip as usual I'm afraid."

"You ought to see mine. World war three wouldn't make as much mess."

"Milk and sugar?"

"Please. Just one sugar. I'm trying to cut it out but can't." Richard sat down on the settee and waited for Damian to appear with the coffee. "This is a lot more civilised than a coffee bar."

"Which one do you go to?" Damian asked as he placed the mugs of coffee on the table, before sitting down next to Richard.

"Axis usually."

"That's where I work. I don't remember seeing you in there."

"I've seen you in there a few times but, it's only really Tuesdays that I go out. It's my day off."

"Mine too. What job do you do?"

"I work at the Tower, taking money at the door. It pays the rent, but not much more than that. I'm getting pissed off with it really, but it is a job after all."

"Yeah, there's not that many about. I was very lucky to get mine. That's where I met Paul."

"Paul? Oh, yes." Damian had mentioned his friend to Richard but not by name. "It was such a shock to us all."

"You knew Paul?"

"Only briefly. I had met him a couple of times or rather, had been introduced to him. A great bloke."

"Yeah. Still, life has to go on." There was a silence during which Damian tried to pluck up the courage to tell Richard of his status. He knew that they would end up in bed together that afternoon, so without thinking, reached into his pocket for the condoms and put them on the table. "You'll have to use one of them."

"Oh." Richard was surprised. Although he fancied Damian something rotten, the forwardness of his new found friend startled him. "Yes. Well. I'd very much like to but, there's something that I must tell you first."

"Well," said Damian plucking up courage; "I've got something to tell you."

"Can I speak honestly Damian?"

"Yes."

"And in total confidence?"

"Yes."

"I don't really like using those but I have to. This is difficult and you'll probably throw me out but, I'm HIV positive."

"So am I Richard, so don't worry."

"You are?"

"Yes. I bought those today. I hate the damn things. I've never bought any before and only used one once."

"Well, as we're both the same, why bother. The damage has been done."

"Quite. Come on, the bedrooms this way."

Fourteen

Damian led Richard into the bedroom, making sure that the door was closed behind him. The last thing that he wanted was to be disturbed. Brushing past Richard, he slowly closed the curtains, removed his shoes and then, lay fully clothed on the bed. Richard at first wasn't sure what to do, but as he began to undo his shirt, Damian shook his head but held a hand out to him. He had no intention of rushing the proceedings or making things easy for either of them.

Richard lay down on the bed next to Damian who put his arms around him in order that their lips would meet for a very lengthy kiss. With one arm holding Richard very close to him, his other hand was very busy first rubbing his friends crotch and then proceeding to continue the undoing of Richard's shirt. Richard slipped his shoes off ready for his jeans to be removed.

Before Damian acceded to Richard's wishes, he placed the older lads hand on his own shirt in order that his torso too, may be exposed. As they lay there caressing each other, it was clear that they were both in for much pleasure. After finding Richard's right nipple and sucking quite heavily on it, he allowed his other hand to wander down Richard's torso until his belt could be felt. A few seconds manipulation and it was undone together with his jeans. Damian couldn't resist the temptation any longer, and as he allowed his hand to explore the inside of Richard's jeans, he felt his own belt being undone and, jeans likewise.

The kissing and caressing continued until Richard grabbed Damian by the waist, pulling him onto himself, allowing him to slide those infuriating jeans and

underpants down to Damian's ankles. He kicked them off and then repeated the process so that Richard too was left only wearing his socks.

"Disappointed?" he asked Richard.

"Definitely not," he said releasing his grip on Damian to give him head. "Are you?" he later enquired coming up for air.

"No way. Bring that here." Richard turned around so that they could both taste the other. After a few minutes of sucking and both of them allowing their fingers to wander to the others hot hole, Damian said, "age before beauty. You want it. Take it. It's yours." Richard didn't need a second invitation and turning Damian onto his front, inserted himself into Damian's hot hole.

"You're so horny," Richard confessed as he continued to pound Damian's arse.

"I'm not the only one. Don't forget that your arse is as eager as mine, and I want it, so don't think you're going to get away with it."

"I wouldn't want to."

It didn't take Richard long before he couldn't help exploding into Damian who by now was nearly cuming himself. He turned Damian onto his back and after sucking his throbbing tool, impaled himself on it.

"Ride 'em cowboy," Damian said excitedly. After no more than a minute, the deed was done and the two boys laid next to each other on the bed

Richard began to stroke Damian's chest and massaging his nipples, with only the occasional stray to his pubic region. Damian knew that there was much more on offer so, after giving Richard another lengthy kiss, reached over and slapped him on his bare arse.

"What was that for?" he asked.

"Just seeing if it was ready for another

pounding!"

"You are horny."

"It's you that's making me horny, and you've just woken it up. That only means one thing."

"What's that?" Richard asked teasingly.

"Doggy style!"

As soon as Damian had said it, he jumped up from the bed and as Richard adopted the position, forgot about teasing his hole first but went straight in. He knew that he too would have to adopt the position later but now, it was his turn and fucked like he'd never fucked before. It wasn't long before he again allowed his fountain of youth to explode into Richard's hot arse. When Damian had separated, Richard quickly turned him over onto his back.

"Woof?" Damian said in his newly found cheeky manner.

"No. Not this time. I want to see you wear earrings."

"Wear what?"

"Earrings."

"But I haven't got any."

"Oh yes you have." Richard grabbed Damian's ankles. "They're called feet." With one gesture, positioned one foot by each of Damian's ears and with the young arse quite visible, quickly fucked it as hard as he could.

Being the second time in quick succession, it was almost six minutes later before Richard managed to empty himself after which, he lay on the bed next to Damian.

"How was that?"

"I felt that."

"It didn't hurt, did it?"

"No, I just got more pleasure from it. That's all."

Not bothering to dress, Damian went into the kitchen, only to return to the bedroom with two mugs of coffee, which the lads drank with their bodies entwined.

"Are you pleased that we met?"

"You bet. I did look for you at the cemetery, but must have missed you."

"You know, I thought that you were going to walk right past me in the street."

"I didn't know that it was you. From the back it did but I couldn't see your face and didn't want to speak, in case it wasn't. That's why I dropped my keys."

"Yeah. That was a bit obvious."

"Sorry."

"Oh. I'm not complaining. If I hadn't called you over then, we wouldn't be here now. I'm glad that I did."

"So am I."

Richard explained that he would need to go back to the flat soon, so after showering and getting dressed, he left. This left Damian with his thoughts. Could there perhaps be a life after Paul? Surely there would have to be some light at the end of his rainbow. It was just a shame that Richard had to leave. Perhaps it was just too early to ask him to stay over.

Damian had managed by bedtime, to persuade himself that whilst he liked Richard very much, and judging by that afternoons steamy session, there would be no problem with the sex; love was not there. Oh, how he wished that it could have been love at first sight, as it had been with Paul. Yes, he was very fond of Richard but despite all of that, he did not know how Richard felt about him. Knowing his luck, the thought; Richard only wanted

him for the sex and nothing more. All he could do was to wait and see. The last thing that he intended was to rush into anything that he might at a later date, regret. After all, they could just remain good friends with, yes, the occasional trips to the bedroom when both were willing.

The next day, Damian went to work as usual and although he did seem to be preoccupied, it wasn't as bad as it had been with Paul. Three days passed and no sign of Richard. Now he knew that their friendship would be just sexual because surely if Richard had have been interested, he would have made contact by now. He did know where he lived and could have called round. Perhaps he had and Damian had not been there. This gave him nothing but ammunition to back up his negative thinking about the whole situation.

The Sunday had been quite a busy day in the coffee bar and Damian was quite pleased to finish at six-thirty. He bade everyone farewell, put on his coat and left for the solitude of his flat. As he approached his flat, he could see someone sitting outside on the wall. His heart jumped a couple of beats in the hope that this was Richard and as he got nearer, he knew that it was.

"Hi love," he said almost running across the road. "Been waiting long?"

"About half an hour."

"Sorry, I had to do an extra half an hour. Come on up." Damian quickly fumbled for his keys and eventually, they were inside Damian's flat. Under normal circumstances, he would have kissed Richard firmly on the lips once they were inside, but something told him not to give his usual greeting on this occasion. He thought that by the expression on Richard's face that he was the bearer of a 'Dear John' letter and that it was all over between them. Preparing himself for the worst, he made coffee and

the two lads sat down in the lounge.

"Did you have a good day?" Richard enquired somewhat sedately.

"Not bad. Busy. What about you?"

"Bloody awful! Still, it's the last."

"You've not been fired?"

"Yeah. Suddenly, I don't fit in with the image that the Tower is hoping to give to its customers. Perhaps I'm too camp, I don't know. Nearly half the staff are gay, so it's not that reason, and I do my job very well."

"Oh shit. What are you going to do now?"

"I don't know. It's come as such a shock that I don't know what to do. I went down to the job centre to sign on. I just caught them before they closed. Since then I've just been walking about."

"Why didn't you come down to the coffee bar? I'd have stood you a coffee."

"I didn't want to disturb you. If I'd have told you at work then, well. They may not like you getting that involved with the customers, and I wouldn't want you to lose your job."

Damian put his arm around Richard and gave him a long kiss. Now he knew that Richard's apparent depression wasn't down to him, especially judging by the reaction to that long welcoming kiss.

"Cheer up, something is bound to turn up. They're even looking for staff at Bodgers. We could always go up there after we've eaten and showered."

"I've never worked in a pub before. I wouldn't know where to start."

"Look. I'll get us something to eat and then we'll shower and go up there. Even if you hate it, it'll keep you going until something else comes along."

"That's true."

"What's your favourite?"

"Mine? Oh, I'll eat anything, but don't worry about me, just get yourself something."

"You'll have something to eat and like it. Yeah?"

"OK. If you insist but, I'll buy the beer later."

"Deal. Ham egg and chips all right?"

"Yeah.   Apart from roast pork and bacon sandwiches, I live on that."

"So do I.   Look.   It won't take long so, why don't you get yourself a shower. I'm not saying that you need one or anything, but you're still wearing your work things and I'll find you something of mine that you can wear tonight."

With Richard ordered to the shower, Damian went into the kitchen to prepare their meal.   Ideally, for their first meal together, Damian would've liked to have done something special, but as he switched on the deep fat fryer and filled it with frozen chips, he thought well, perhaps the basic will suffice.   He could always prepare a proper meal for the two of them next Tuesday when he would have more time.   As he heard the shower stop, he served the food onto two plates and took it through into the lounge.

"It's ready," he shouted. "Don't be long."

"Ok."

"Just put a robe on. You can dry off later."

Richard did as he was instructed and wearing nothing but a bath robe, walked into the lounge to enjoy his meal. Damian had switched the television on and was checking teletext to get the news which they both watched as they ate. Afterwards, Damian showered and then came into the lounge wearing only a skimpy towel.

"Come on through," he said; "and, I'll dry your

back if you dry mine." Richard needed no further invitation and promptly followed Damian into the bedroom. As Richard turned round so that his back could be dried, he couldn't help noticing the fact that Damian was getting erect. As he lowered the bath robe to the floor and felt Damian's hands over his back, he responded likewise, turning around in order to remove Damian's towel, and as he dropped to his knees, he drew his new found love towards him.

It was almost an hour later when the two lads showered for the second time and then dressed. Neither had intended for another steamy sex session but conversely, neither tried very hard to resist the temptation. Once ready, they left for Bodgers. Richard lit cigarettes for both of them as they walked along the road and once into Cookson Street, he grabbed Damian's hand and after kissing him firmly on the lips, kept hold of it until they arrived. The doubts that Damian had been having disappeared as a result of this loving gesture and began to swing arms as they walked along.

Once inside Bodgers, pints in hand, Damian asked if the manager was about and explained that Richard was looking for a job because he had just been made redundant. He didn't want to say that Richard had been sacked, just in case it prejudiced his chances. When the manager came down, he took Richard to one corner of the pub and they chatted for what seemed to Damian to be hours but, was in reality, no more than twenty minutes. When he came back Damian pounced on Richard to ask him how the interview went.

"I start tomorrow. Twelve until six."

"Great! Another pint to celebrate then."

"It's only a trial, just to see how I get on."

"You'll soon pick it up. Pulling pints can't be

that difficult and once you get to know where everything is, you'll be fine."

"I hope you're right."

The two of them sat down to consume their celebratory pint and following several more - all in a good cause - they left for Damian's flat.

"Thanks love," Richard said as they got to the downstairs door. "I really appreciate it." He began to do up his coat.

"Where are you going?"

"Home. Why?"

"Nothing." Damian felt very disappointed. He had hoped that Richard would stay the night, but hadn't of course asked him. Richard wouldn't be that presumptuous. "Coffee?"

"Yeah. OK then."

Once inside the flat, coffee was procured and Damian stood looking at Richard.

"Why haven't you taken your coat off," he said making his way to join him on the settee. "Where do you think you'll be sleeping tonight?"

"Oh." This took Richard aback. "Here?"

"Too right. You can start with your coat and I'll help you with the rest. Come on. Bring your coffee."

Damian again led Richard into the bedroom. Both of them had drank too much to make staying over anything other than a time for sleeping, but the morning would yield something different.

Damian woke just before eight and carefully crept out of bed in order to make coffee for both him and Richard. He carefully placed a mug of coffee on the bedside table and as he did so, he felt Richard's hand cupping his balls. Quickly putting down his own coffee, he leapt on the bed and cuddled up to Richard who by

now, was more than eager for what was about to follow.

The two lads just couldn't get enough of each other. Their affection for each other was also beginning to increase. When they had finished their latest session, they both gazed into each others eyes. Damian was beginning to fall in love with Richard. The feelings were very similar to those that he had experienced with Paul. He knew that it was much more than a pure lust or sexual attraction. At the same time, whilst he realised that Richard must be very fond of him, nothing direct had been said to indicate to Damian that phase two of their relationship had been completed, and that he was ready for phase three.

Damian too wasn't sure whether or not he was ready for the ultimate move. Oh yes, their friendship was great and their sex life fantastic but he knew deep down only too well that he couldn't go through another bereavement. They were both HIV positive yes. The chance of either of them dying prematurely from AIDS was quite high, even though that could in itself be years away. He needed to know more about Richard's illness so that he could determine the possibility of advancing their relationship, or at the very least, offering to go to those heights. Then he came down to earth.

Very few gay relationships lasted more than five or six years. Almost everyone that he had spoken to about the subject was on their second or third long term relationship. They do break down. Pressure of those people on the scene who seem to be hell bent on separating a couple, accidentally meeting someone who they love more than their present partner, or just complete incompatibility after living together for a few months. He wanted none of this and knew that because of their status, casual sex or clandestine meetings would be totally out of

the question for either of them. Was he brave enough to make that move?

It was when Richard said that he thought he ought to be going that Damian responded.

"Why don't you stay for a day or so. You're more than welcome to do so."

"You're very kind and I'd love to, but I would be imposing. You don't really want me clogging up your life, do you?"

"I might."

"And I might want to but-----."

"Then when we're dressed, we'll go back to your place and you can get a change of clothes. Where's the problem?"

"I don't know, really."

"Well then." Damian was determined.

"It's just that, this place is so nice."

"And your bedsit isn't?"

"It's more like a tip than anything else. I'd feel embarrassed about taking anyone back there. You know?"

"Well, if that's the only reason, I can always wait outside."

"Oh, I wouldn't want you to do that. You'll just have to take it as you find it."

"That's OK. Don't worry about it. This place ain't a palace."

"It is compared to mine. It's so big."

"What are we talking about now? The flat or other things!"

"Perhaps both!"

The lads got dressed and made their way to Richard's bedsit. It was as he had described. A very small room and although it did have a separate toilet and kitchen, once the bed was folded down from the wall, you

could only just walk around it. There was no heating other than a one bar electric fire which looked as if it came out of the ark, and the room was very cold and damp. Richard was clearly embarrassed about the state of the place and it took Damian all of his time not to pass any comment, or to look too disgusted. Clearly, Richard was not going to be the world's tidiest man, but perhaps he could mould him as time goes on. He would see how they got on during Richard's short stay. If the boot were on the other foot, he would certainly be on his best behaviour during an initial trial period, but what would happen afterwards.

Other than the fold down bed, there was only a wardrobe come dressing table and if he was honest, he wouldn't have been able to get half of his clothes in it and perhaps would have to resort to piles of clothes on the floor. His would however be organised.

"Calm down," Damian said as Richard seemed to be running around the room like a headless chicken; "there's no rush."

"I know but, I just need to get out of here."

"Well, I don't think that I could live in a place like this. It's very small."

"Yeah. Now you know why I could never bring anyone back here. I hate the place really but, I needed my independence and well, it does serve its purpose." Richard zipped up his bag. "Ready. Let's go."

Fifteen

The two lads walked arm in arm during the twenty minute journey back to Damian's flat. They were totally ignorant of people looking at them, or the occasional 'tutting' that they experienced as they passed people in the street. With Blackpool being the gay capital of the north, the local people had become used to having gay people about but very few would ever tolerate people walking arm in arm together or even holding hands. Even members of the gay community itself, frowned upon such activity. Being out and proud was one thing, but there was perhaps a time and a place for their current behaviour. Within the confines of any of the gay bars, nobody would bat an eyelid, and would not be interested in how people behaved at home. Out in the street was something that even the gay community was only slowly getting used to.

For many, it was the fear of being recognised. Some people were openly gay within the scene but didn't want the whole world to know about it. Fear of perhaps having to walk home alone in the early hours of the morning and being attacked. A reality, sadly.

This was why when the bumped into Tony a couple of hundred yards from the flat, he reacted in the way that he did. Instead of speaking to either of them, he promptly crossed the road not ten feet in front of them and walked by on the other side of the road. This upset Damian but he could tell that Tony's face was trying to tell him something, and at a later date, would have to find out what that was.

As he approached the flat, the action of separating from Richard in order to get his keys out of his pocket, prompted him to realise that unintentionally, their

arm in arm stroll had continued the whole way home and not just down the stairs from Richard's bedsit. He smiled to himself a rather cheeky smile that made Richard too realise just exactly what they had done.

"Bloody hell," Richard said as he closed the main door behind him. "We haven't, we didn't."

"We did and I don't care." Damian raced up the stairs to open the flat door. "We're not married yet so you can carry yourself over the threshold." Richard tapped him gently on that lovely arse of his and closed the flat door. Once inside he pulled Damian towards him and kissed him lovingly, hardly coming up for air during its ten minute duration.

Damian held Richard by the hand and led him into the bedroom. This time it would be for more mundane matters than sex. He opened the empty drawer in his chest of drawers and the one side of the wardrobe that was empty.

"There you go. Put your clothes away, make yourself at home and I'll go and get the coffee."

Richard neatly folded his clothes and half filled the small drawer that Damian had opened for him. Using the spare coat hangers that were there, his jeans, best trousers and four shirts were hung. They were quite creased from the journey and the laxidasical way that Richard tended to treat his clothes but after all, he could always iron them before wearing them.

During the next three days both Richard and Damian acted as if they had been 'married' for many years. They began to realise that they both had some bad points and that they would have to compromise quite considerably if they were to get together on a full time basis.

Damian would go to work each day, returning

between half past six and seven o'clock in the evening, only to find that behind that quiet and loving exterior, beated the heart of a fairly good cook. A meal would be waiting for him and during the day, Richard put on the metaphoric apron and did whatever housework was required. There were however the down sides.

Richard's bad habit of throwing his clothes on the floor as they were discarded them for either a shower or for bed. Damian refused to pick them up but kept dropping hints to Richard in the hope that he would improve. Damian's bad habit of leaving the washing up undone and throwing the scatter cushions from the settee to the floor annoyed Richard. They would discuss their failings and as the days went on, gradually got better. Their bond strengthened and Richard's four day stay stretched to two weeks. By that time they were inseparable. Bonded together in much the same way that Damian and Paul had been.

With the initial problems ironed out it became very clear to both of the lads that a short period of separation was needed for both of them to gather their thoughts and feelings, perhaps in the cold light of day rather than whilst fucking each other something rotten. To that end, Richard left after the two weeks and it was left that Richard would call into the Axis coffee bar after a few days.

That night, Tony called round to see Damian.

"Hi love. Sorry I haven't been round, but you know how it is. I didn't want to interrupt anything."

"You wouldn't have been interrupting anything. Anyway. We would have found bath robes or something."

"Well. How's it going?"

"I'm not sure."

"You're not sure? Blimey! He's been here for

two weeks. You must've got down to it at some stage."

"Yeah. I mean, when I weren't at work."

"Mind if I get a coffee?"

"No. Help yourself. The machine's on."

Tony went into the kitchen and returned shortly afterwards with a large mug of coffee. As he came back into the lounge, it looked as if Damian was about to cry. He was obviously very upset about something.

"Where is Richard?"

"He's gone back home for a few days."

"Why?"

"Well, we were talking last night about us, about what's happened, and he said that it might be better for him to spend a few nights at home. He thought that it would give us both a bit of breathing space. We've been in each others pockets for the whole time, apart from working. I don't know. Perhaps he's having second thoughts."

"I doubt it."

"What makes you say that? The guy's absolutely besotted with you. He's not having second thoughts, he's just giving you a bit of space to come to your senses and to ask him to move in."

"Do you really think so?"

"You asked me that when you and Paul got together. Of course I think so. It's quite usual for one partner to move out for a period. It's just etiquette. He may well need time to think about whether you are the one for him but what's more important than that; is he the one for you?"

"I'd like to think so. Even if he does leave his dirty clothes all over the flat."

"All over the flat, or just in the bedroom."

"Just in the bedroom. Do you really think that's

why he's gone?"

"Yes. I've done it in the past. What time did he leave?"

"About sixish, why?"

"And when are you seeing him again?"

"I don't know. He's going to call down to the coffee bar."

Tony and Damian chatted well into the early hours. Had Damian forgotten completely all that they had spoken about when Paul first came on the scene, or had the love that clearly existed between the two lads blinded him from seeing straight.

It was almost three o'clock when Tony finally left Damian to think about his future. As he closed Damian's flat door, he glanced down the stairs and saw what he thought was a figure standing by the front door. Because the main stairs light was off, he could see the figure quite clearly and decided to pluck up enough courage to go downstairs to see who it was.

"Who's there?" he said almost whispering.

"Me," came the reply. "It's me." This totally bemused Tony.

"Who's me?"

"Richard." Tony immediately opened the door.

"What are you doing here? Come on up to my flat." He took Richard up to his flat and sat him down. "Well. What's going on?"

"I'm sorry, I didn't mean to wake you up."

"You didn't. I've been in with Damian. What's the problem?"

"I love him. I really do. I just couldn't face staying in the bedsit without him."

"Have you told him that you love him?"

"No. I don't even know why I suggested that

we should part for a few days. Bloody stupid, but I don't think that I can live without him anymore."

"Well, if that's the case you'd better go and tell him yourself."

"I know but it's so late and I know he's got quite a heavy day tomorrow at work. I didn't want to wake him."

"Were you going to stay out there all night?"

"I don't know. I got back to the bedsit, threw my stuff onto the bed and came back. I really can't live without him. It is stupid isn't it."

"No. I don't think that that's stupid. What I do think is stupid is that you haven't said anything to him about how you feel."

"I know. I have wanted to, but I suppose that I didn't want him to take pity on me or anything like that."

"Pity? He's as much in love with you as you are with him. Don't you know that either? Surely you must have guessed."

"I thought that he was very interested in me, but I didn't know that he loved me as much as I love him."

"There's only one thing that you can do. Come with me." Tony took Richard to Damian's door. "Now. I'll ring the bell and when he opens the door, you go ahead and tell him that you love him. Ok?"

"Ok."

Richard stood outside the door and when he had composed himself, nodded to Tony who rang Damian's door bell. As the light came on, Tony went back into his flat, leaving Richard standing there. Damian opened the door.

"Richard!" he exclaimed throwing his arms around him.

"I love you Damian. I really do."

"And I love you too. Come in." The two of them hugged each other in the hall during which the tears well and truly flowed. They kissed and after Damian had managed to remove Richard's coat, led him into the bedroom without saying another word. Richard sat down on the bed and then held both of Damian's hands.

"I'm sorry love, but we've got to talk."

"What about?"

"Us. We've got to decide where we're going."

"What made you come back so quickly?"

"I love you and I just can't live without you. Not anymore. I only wish that my place was bigger because I'd ask you to move in with me."

"What's wrong with this place?"

"Nothing. Why?"

"Well, why don't you move in here? There's plenty of room and I would like that very much."

"Are you sure?"

"Of course I'm sure. I really love you too you know. I didn't want you to go. I don't know what I thought, but after you went, the place felt just so empty. It was then I knew that I not only want you in here, but I want you for life."

"Is that a proposal?"

"Yeah. If you like."

"And you accept?"

"Of course I do. Now keep that quiet," Damian said touching Richard on the lips; "and just open it wide."

Damian dropped his jeans to the floor. His erection was plain to see. As Richard sucked hard on Damian's throbbing meat, both of the lads began to cry again. A quick lick of Damian's balls was followed by more head as a finger slid gently inside him. Making no noise but taking off the remainder of his clothes ready to

wear his feet as earrings, waited patiently for Richard to expose himself and to satisfy his Damian's ultimate desire. Richard had only just cum when Damian grabbed him and quickly sliding off the bed, knelt behind him so that he too could give his lover, something that he had made himself.

Satisfaction both given and received, the two lads collapsed on the bed. It was almost eleven o'clock the following morning when the woke. Richard woke first and decided that after a call of nature, he would surprise Damian by making the coffee and slipping it onto his bedside cabinet without waking him. Having accomplished this, he went round to his own side of the bed as if nothing had happened. When Damian finally woke, he turned over and thought to himself that Richard was still asleep. Then he noticed the coffee on Richard's bedside cabinet. Thinking that it had gone cold, he got out of bed and picked up the mug of coffee that Richard had put there for him. Realising that it could have only been there a matter of minutes, crept back into bed and began to kiss Richard tenderly on the back of the neck and shoulders.

"Good morning," Richard said responding to the affection that was being showed to him.

"Morning angel," Damian replied. "How long have you been awake?"

"About half an hour. Why?"

"Well, one good turn deserves another," he said as he allowed his left hand to wander down to Richard's crotch. Realising that Richard was already hard to the touch he said; "I hope you were thinking about me," and before Richard could answer, went down on him ensuring that breakfast was quickly dispensed into him. When Damian too was relieved of the contents of his own throbbing tool, they decided that whilst they would like to

stay in bed all day, that Richard would have to go and get the rest of his possessions from his bedsit. Before doing that, Richard felt that he must ask about the conversation that they'd had in the early hours of the morning, just in case he had been dreaming.

"Damian," he said pulling him down onto the settee in the lounge. "Were you serious last night when you asked me to stay? I mean, you weren't just saying that?"

"Of course I wasn't. After the second time that we met, I knew that I was falling in love with you and that I wanted you to come and live here. I just didn't know just how to say it."

"Why not?"

"I don't know. You're very much like Paul and perhaps I needed time to see you for who you are and not as a clone of Paul's."

"And have you now seen me for what I am?"

"Yes. You hadn't been gone more than an hour before I realised that it was you that I wanted."

"And Paul?"

"The memories will always be there, but I've stopped comparing you with him now. I wondered if my attraction to you was because of that. Now I know that it wasn't. That's why I didn't ask you before."

"Yes. I can understand that. I've fallen deeply in love with you. Love at first sight, if you like. That first day we met in the bus shelter at the cemetery. I could have given you one there and then."

"Why didn't you?"

"Because of my status. If I wasn't HIV positive then I would have done."

"Even if I was?"

"That wouldn't have made any difference, even

now. If I wasn't positive and you were, I would still want to have you, be with you, to love you. It's not that important even though yes, you could have passed it onto me. Love is more important than a virus. We'd found ways around that for the sex side. Wouldn't we."

"Yes." He paused for a moment. "So, do you still want to move in?"

"Too right. Try and stop me."

"In that case," he said reaching over to the top drawer of the wall unit; "you'll need these. They're the keys to this place, and we'll need to get your stuff over here."

Richard gave Damian one last kiss before the two of them set off with a bag full of empty carrier bags for Richard's bedsit. It took them most of the afternoon to pack up all of Richard's possessions and to ferry them back to Damian's flat. Thankfully, Richard travelled fairly light. He carried the heavy things like his music centre and speakers while Damian would carry bags containing tapes, clothes and the few personal items that Richard managed to collect during his life to date.

Where they would all go would be a different story but, they knew that they would enjoy the prospect of finding a home for everything, and everything would be in its rightful place.

About seven o'clock that evening came the first trial that their relationship would have to endure. They decided that they would go out for a drink and something to eat. Having decided to have something special, they made their way to a fairly new Indian restaurant near the suburb of Bispham, a matter of twenty-five minutes walk away from the flat, out of Blackpool. They asked for a table for two and ordered their initial drinks.

Damian had his back to the three tables that

were already occupied and after Richard had put down his menu, they ordered their meal. Richard noticed that one of the lads sitting at a corner table kept looking across as if he may have known either of the two lads. This unnerved Richard because as the lad walked back from paying a call of nature, he began to head for the table that Damian and he were occupying. He stood about eight feet away from the table and then called over to the manager.

"How long have you been serving these?" he asked aggressively.

"I don't know what you mean sir," the Manager replied.

"Fucking queers with AIDS."

"They are only having a meal sir, nothing more. Please return to your seat."

"Throw them out."

"No sir. They have done nothing wrong."

"But," he said pointing to Richard; "he's got AIDS."

"I have not," Richard replied.

"My mates and I know you and we know that you've got it. Why don't you just fuck off and leave everybody alone. You shouldn't be allowed out."

"Calm down sir," the manager said. "Carry on with your meal. Please sit down."

Eventually, the lad returned to his table having caused the greatest amount of embarrassment that he could have done. Defiantly and despite the constant jibes that lasted all through Damian and Richard's meal, they were served and after their sweat, decided not to stay for coffee, and to make a fairly quick getaway.

The last thing that they wanted was any aggravation from another group of gay lads because, while they had been sitting there, Richard recognised the loud

mouthed git that had been speaking to them. As they approached the sanctuary of their flat, they sat down on a bench. Richard was visibly shaking.

"Did you know those guys?"

"Yeah. The bastards are gay and the one that was mouthing off was at the clinic the same time that I got my test result. He's a real sod."

"But if he's gay, why make all that fuss?"

"They do. They are gay themselves, but enjoy giving grief to anyone who's positive. They're bastards. Nothing more."

"Yeah, but surely the gay community are behind those of us who are positive. We're all gay."

"I know that, but it's not the case. They are people who go out cottaging, looking for chicken sex because anyone else that they fancy might be positive. They're gay but not prepared to behave. It's just another version of queer bashing. That's all."

"It stinks. I could never do anything like that."

"Neither could I." They hugged each other.

"Come on Damian. Let's go and have a drink."

Sixteen

The incident in the restaurant bothered Damian. He knew that there were plenty of queer bashers about but had never thought that some of them might be gay. It played on his mind quite a lot as he looked at each customer who came into the coffee bar. Mind you, the only places that he felt safe were either at work, at a Body Positive meeting, or at home. Home he knew was the safest place. He never said anything to Richard about it because he didn't mainly want to show his ignorance about such matters.

The weeks went by and soon he and Richard's half year anniversary came around. The gay community is probably the only one that celebrates such events but in many cases would parallel a five year affair within the heterosexual community. Therefore, something special needed to be done.

Damian didn't have a clue how to surprise Richard, other than to buy him a nice present, so in the end, Damian decided upon a Chinese meal at a local restaurant that they had come to know very well. Indeed, in their first six months together, many chicken and prawn balls had been consumed by the pair, once they had been heavily doused in a sweet and sour sauce.

By now, Damian had turned eighteen and in every sense of the word, was now legal. He would make a point of ordering drinks in Bodgers, once of course he had shown them his birth certificate to prove that he was of age. He still looked very young, almost as young as he had been when he first set out from his home in Coventry. Shaving was now on the menu for the mornings, not every morning but perhaps twice or occasionally three times a

week.

After the meal, Richard left the table to pay a call of nature and on his return, stopped to talk to one of the waiters. Damian could not see the conversation because his back was facing them. Richard returned with a grin that the Cheshire cat would have been proud of. This intrigued Damian who couldn't resist the temptation to ask about it.

"It was a good meal."

"Yes. Always is but, tonight I'm paying."

"You can't. You're not working yet."

"I can. I've been saving up some out of my giro ready for tonight."

"Is that why you're beaming?"

"Partly." Damian was now even more intrigued as their conversation was interrupted by the waiter arriving at their table with a bottle of Champagne and two glasses.

"Richard. We can't afford this."

"We can. Tonight is our six month anniversary. Money is no object."

"I thought you'd forgotten."

"How could I ever forget the last six months! I knew that when you suggested a meal out that you may have thought that I'd forgot. Well, I haven't."

"But Champagne?"

"Damian, listen." Richard opened the bottle and poured out two glasses. He put one down in front of Damian, the other in front of himself. "I want you to play a game."

"A game? Here?"

"Yes, here."

"Ok."

"Good. Now before we drink the Champagne, hold out your hand and close your eyes."

"What?"

"Hold out your hand and close your eyes."

"Here?"

"Yes.   Stop asking questions and do it." Damian did as Richard had asked him to do. As he did so, he felt Richard put something into his hand. "Happy anniversary."

"Can I open my eyes yet?"

"Not quite."   Richard carefully left his seat, moved around the table to Damian's side and knelt down. "Right. You can open your eyes providing that you marry me."

Damian didn't know what to say as he slowly opened his eyes. He saw Richard kneeling down at the side of him and in his hand was a small box. Still shell-shocked and saying nothing, he slowly opened the box. Inside was a signet ring. Damian's face was a picture. Totally gobsmacked and shocked. As Damian looked at Richard, he took the ring and placed it on Damian's third finger of his left hand.

"I mean it Damian. Will you marry me?" The tears began to gush down Damian's face. He took a swig of Champagne, coughed and then opened his mouth all to no avail. No words came out. He just couldn't believe that Richard had stolen his thunder. "Well?"

"Well, yes. Of course I will." They hugged each other in the middle of the restaurant totally oblivious to the other people around them. When they had released each other sufficiently for Damian to reach into his left jacket pocket, he produced an identical box to that which Richard had given him. He gave it to Richard and when he had opened it, Damian placed it firmly on the third finger of Richard's hand. More hugs and kisses followed. The Champagne drunk, they left the restaurant for

Bodgers, where they saw the night away in total oblivion to anyone around them. Their love for each other was the only thing that mattered to them.

The next day, Damian went to work as usual, proudly displaying the signet ring that he had been given the previous evening. There for the entire world to see. He hadn't been there for very long before Richard came down for a coffee. Although the owners of the coffee bar had noticed that Damian was now sporting a new piece of jewellery, no comment was made to him about it. When during a quiet moment Damian and Richard sat at the same table, Richard's ring too was there for all to see. Andrew could not resist any longer. He went out into the kitchen and peering around the corner began to hum the wedding march, not loud, but loud enough so that Richard and Damian could hear.

"Congratulations," he said as the two love birds looked up. "And about time too."

"Thanks Andy. I thought you hadn't noticed."

"Hadn't noticed? You've been putting your hand in front of my face all morning. Of course I noticed. When's the big day?"

"I don't know. Richard and I haven't decided that yet."

"Let's have a proper look then." Andrew bent over to the table and examined both the lads' rings carefully. "Did you know?"

"No. Richard asked me in the restaurant last night. I wouldn't mind, but, I was going to ask him."

"Yeah. I stole his thunder a bit."

"It's funny that both rings match."

"Do they?" Damian hadn't realised that. Both the lads had bought the rings on separate occasions and had each bought an identical ring. Damian grabbed

Richard's hand and starred at the ring. "They do! I didn't know that. I never realised."

"Neither had I," Richard added. "Perhaps it's an omen."

"Well, I wish you both well. You are well matched and obviously in love so, go for it."

Richard stayed at the coffee bar for the remainder of the day, only briefly leaving in order to sign on. He was away for less than fifteen minutes but to Damian, it may as well as been a lifetime. The two lovebirds walked home holding hands, back to their love nest and to another session of hot steamy sex.

Damian just couldn't wait and had already undone Richard's fly and the top of his jeans before they had opened the door to the flat. He resisted no more as the door was closed behind them and within two minutes, they were completely naked and doing what all good rampant guys do in such circumstances. They play fought around the lounge coffee table to see who was going to get fucked first. Damian in the end got his wish and after making sure that Richard's cock was nice and moist, assumed the position.

About two weeks after their engagement, they were playing pool at Bodgers when someone in the bar shouted; "I know that arse." Both of them looked around despite the fact that it was Richard who was bent over the pool table at the time.

"Ben!" he exclaimed. "What are you doing here?"

"Just eyeing up the local talent. You haven't changed. Still the old queen that you were. Is this your latest conquest?"

"That's Damian, yes."

"Still into chicken then."

"Ignore him Damian. He was born with his mouth and arse in the wrong places."

"Cheeky. Mind you, I wouldn't mind a slice of that myself. Nice basket."

"Damian and I are together. What we had is over, and I'd rather not talk to you, so if you don't mind, why don't you just piss off and leave us alone."

"Another one night stand, no doubt. Yeah. I'll leave you alone, for now." The mouthy lad went up the other end of the pub.

"Who was that?"

"That's Ben. He and I used to have something going."

"How long did it last?"

"About four months. As soon as he realised that he'd given me the virus, he pissed off. Thank goodness. He's trouble Damian. Just ignore him."

"Too right." Damian kissed Richard as if to say, 'just remember who you do love and what's in the past should stay there.' "Anyway, it's your shot."

Although Damian seemed concerned at the time, he didn't really take Ben's sudden arrival as anything other than what it was. A trouble maker looking for more. By now he knew Richard well enough to know that the arrival of one of his ex's, would do nothing other than to strengthen the relationship that he had with Richard.

Perhaps because of their new found lease of life, they began to mix more with the other regulars and specifically in Damian's case, would flirt with some of the customers at Axis. They both knew that there was nothing involved with their actions and their relationship gained momentum.

The next three months saw their happiness continue and on one of Damien's days off, they decided

that it was time to plan the wedding itself.

"Where are we going to have it?"

"Here?"

"No Damian. This place is ours. Besides that, it's too small. We're going to need somewhere bigger."

"Well, let's see who we're going to invite."

They began to list down their joint friends and acquaintances that each had separately. True most had been introduced to the 'other half,' but perhaps knew one of them better than the other. They began to count the number of names that they had put down.

"Richard, there's nearly eighty people on this list."

"That's what I said. This place is going to be too small."

"We can't have that many. It'll cost us a fortune."

"Let's look at it again. We'll mark the very close friends with the letter 'A', and the others with the letter 'B'. Then what we do is to invite all the 'A's' to the wedding and have something like a disco in the evening for both the 'A's' and the 'B's'."

"Ok."

Eventually, they narrowed the 'A' list down to twenty-two people and began the task of looking for somewhere to hold the event.

"Who's going to do the service?"

"I don't know." They began to look at each other with blank expressions. "I know. Pass me that book Damian." The address book was passed and Richard flicked through it until he found the number that he wanted.

"Who are you looking for?"

"Someone I used to know got married a few

months ago. They're both gay, so I'll phone them to see if they can tell me who did the service."

"But would they do it for us?"

"I don't see why not. Pass the 'phone and I'll call them."

Damian went into the kitchen to make coffee while Richard telephoned the number. By the time he came back, Richard was already talking to the minister. Damian put the coffee down on the coffee table and waited until Richard had finished the conversation.

"Well?" he said excitedly.

"He'll do it. We've got to go and see him tomorrow night about eight and he'll talk to us then."

"Wow!" Getting married had been more of a pipe dream to Damian. This was reality. It would really happen. He remembered back to the words of Smalltown Boy and the other songs that he had listened to on the train from Coventry, especially 'You make me feel (mighty real).' Richard had made him feel mighty real, and he hoped that Richard felt the same as he did.

The next night they both went to see the minister and after discussing their requirements, fixed a date for the proceedings. They explained that at present they hadn't got a venue but that they would get back to him, once of course that one had been booked. That night they went into Bodgers again and spoke to one of the bar staff about their predicament. They wondered if he might be able to suggest any suitable venues.

"Why not here?"

"Here?" Damian had not thought of Bodgers. "But won't you have to stay open?"

"Oh yes, but we've done them before here. It's not usually a problem. We just turn off the music while the service is on. Speak to Chris the manager when he

comes down and see what he says."

"Thanks."

Their discussions with Chris proved successful and after making a quick 'phone call to the minister, just to confirm everything, they agreed to hold the event there. The wedding service would be at four o'clock in the afternoon, and there would be a buffet for about twenty-five to follow. Damian had already spoken to the lads at Axis who had agreed to do all of the catering at cost, providing that the pub didn't have any objection. They didn't. Their other friends would be invited for about seven o'clock in the evening and because there was already going to be an evening disco at the pub, they would not need to pay for that.

They took a leisurely stroll back to the flat and couldn't wait to tell Tony of their plans. As there was no reply from his flat, they would have to wait until the next day so, being quite tired and fairly well drunk went straight to bed. They would need to send out the invitations out in the next day or so in order that they could get answers back for the catering. There would need to be a best man and an usher.

All this went through Damien's mind as he kissed Richard goodnight, turned over and went straight to sleep. There would be so much to do in the next few weeks before their big day and they would both need to get plenty of sleep in order to cope with the excitement that would ensue.

Eventually Friday the twenty-second arrived and the two lads spent the morning getting ready for their big day. Their suits and shirts hung on the back of the bedroom door ready for the afternoon. Damian prepared breakfast while Richard showered.

"Well, today's the day," he said sitting down on

the settee.

"It is. Any regrets?" Damian handed Richard his toast.

"No. You?"

"No. Well, perhaps one." Richard looked up as Damian sat next to him. "Just one."

"What's that?"

"That we hadn't done it before."

"Oh. I was worried then."

"Why? Did you think that I wanted to get rid of you or something? With a dick like that? No way." He began to open Richard's bath robe and to bring him to readiness. "There's no way that this is going anywhere other than in my mouth or up my arse."

"You know that." Richard had to put his toast down on the coffee table. "But if you keep that up something's bound to happen."

"That's the idea."

Damian firmly took hold of Richard hard cock and led him into the bedroom. He sat him down on the bed and opened his robe. Slowly, he let his jeans fall to the floor and without saying a word, pushed his own throbbing tool into Richard's mouth. While Richard was giving head like he had never done before, Damian removed the rest of his clothes. When Richard came up for air, Damian pushed him back on the bed so that his cock was pointing up towards the ceiling. Straddling Richard, he positioned himself so that his lovers cock was only an inch from his still very young tender arse. After sucking hard on Richard's nipples, he knelt up so that he could quickly and easily impale himself on Richard's waiting cock.

Damian bounced happily for about five minutes before he could feel Richard ejaculating inside him. This

time he didn't stop but kept going until Richard had become very hard again. As if by magic, Damian - whose cock had just been drifting in the breeze - shot his load all over Richard, who was not prepared for that to happen.

"That's never happened to me," he said wiping the spunk from his face. "Never."

"Never?"

"No. I've always had to wank it first."

"You obviously hit the right spot then," Damian added before allowing them to separate and to cuddle together on the bed. "Now we both need a shower. You go first."

"I'd have waited if I'd have known," Richard said making his way back into the shower. Once inside, he began to soap himself again. He knew that Damian was waiting outside, so did not completely close the shower curtain. Richard was still erect, having been brought back to life inside his lover and Damian could see this from his vantage point. He waited until Richard had his back to him and then quietly reached into the shower cubicle and began to wank Richard hard. This took Richard by surprise at first, especially when Damian joined him in the shower and quickly put his own cock into Richard's eager arse.

Eventually the lads came out of the shower and continued with their preparations for their wedding. Damian had earlier telephone the minister and Bodgers, just to check on the arrangements. All was well and by the time that Tony rang the door bell at three-thirty, they were ready. Shortly afterwards the taxi arrived and they were soon at Bodgers. As they got out of the taxi, they could see that some of the guests had already arrived. Andrew was standing outside and handed Damian a card.

"Thanks." He kissed Andrew on the lips.

"It's from the three of us," he said.   "Hi Richard."

"Hi."

Once inside, they collected many more cards and a few presents. They still had about ten minutes to spare, so they began to open the cards. When Damian opened the card from the lads at Axis, he got a shock. As well as the card were rail tickets from Blackpool to London, a hotel reservation and one hundred pounds.

"Andrew!" Damian screamed at the top of his voice. He couldn't believe what he had found inside the card. Andrew came over. "What's this?"

"Well, you've been so good at the coffee bar, and we knew that you weren't going away anywhere, so we thought that you ought to have a little honeymoon."

"This is too much."

"No it isn't. You both deserve it."

The minister arrived and the service began. Afterwards they partied into the early hours. The next day they would be off to London, and to the happiness that would ensure for the rest of their lives.

BY THE SAME AUTHOR

THE ELLIOTT HADLEY SERIES

The Korecky Affair
Humphries Paw
The Balls Cross Murders
The al-Jeema File

AUTOBIOGRAPHICAL

My Walk With Christ
Pink Hopscotch*

FOR TEENAGERS

The Mystic Gateway
Adventure at The Bulls Head

*Contains ADULT material